THE D'ARCY DA

across the Oxfordsh and Thames valley

Nick Moon

This guide to the D'Arcy Dalton Way, replacing the original guide written and published by the late Rowland Pomfret on behalf of the Oxford Fieldpaths Society in 1987 and now out of print, describes both the route of the D'Arcy Dalton Way itself and eight circular walks using parts of its route ranging in length from 4.0 to 13.4 miles. The text of the guide to the Way and each circular walk gives details of nearby places of interest and is accompanied by specially drawn maps of the route which also indicate local pubs and a skeleton road network.

The author, Nick Moon, has lived on the Oxfordshire border or regularly visited the county all his life and has, for 25 years, been an active member of the Oxford Fieldpaths Society, which seeks to protect and improve the county's footpath and bridleway network. Thanks to the help and encouragement of the late Don Gresswell MBE, he was introduced to the writing of books of walks and has since written or contributed to a number of publications in this field.

The author and the Executive Committee of the Oxford Fieldpaths Society wish to thank Oxfordshire County Council for their kind cooperation in organising the acquisition and erection of special signposts for the D'Arcy Dalton Way to coincide with the publication of this book and for their help in tackling obstructions and other problems found while surveying the Way itself and the eight circular walks.

O·F·S

OTHER PUBLICATIONS BY NICK MOON

Family Walks
Family Walks 1 :   Chilterns - South : Book Castle 1997
Family Walks 2 :   Chilterns - North : Book Castle 1998

Chiltern Walks Trilogy
Chiltern Walks 1:   Hertfordshire, Bedfordshire and
                      North Buckinghamshire:
                      Book Castle (new edition) 1996
Chiltern Walks 2 :   Buckinghamshire:
                      Book Castle (new edition) 1997
Chiltern Walks 3 :   Oxfordshire and West Buckinghamshire:
                      Book Castle (new edition) 1996

Oxfordshire Walks
Oxfordshire Walks 1: Oxford, The Cotswolds and The Cherwell
                     Valley: Book Castle (new edition) 1998
Oxfordshire Walks 2: Oxford, The Downs and The Thames Valley:
                     Book Castle 1995

Other Complete Books
Walks for Motorists: Chilterns (Southern Area):
                      Frederick Warne 1979
Walks for Motorists: Chilterns (Northern Area):
                      Frederick Warne 1979
Walks in the Hertfordshire Chilterns: Shire 1986

First published October 1999
by The Book Castle
12 Church Street, Dunstable, Bedfordshire.

© Nick Moon, 1999

Printed in Great Britain by Antony Rowe Ltd., Chippenham, Wilts.

ISBN 1 871 199 34 4

Contents

Acknowledgements

The author wishes to acknowledge with grateful thanks all the work and enthusiasm of Alison Kemp and the late Rowland Pomfret and Stephen Kemp in the mid-1980s without which the D´Arcy Dalton Way would not have been established and this book would not have been possible.

Cover photograph: Approaching Broadwell (Map 12).
© Nick Moon.

3

OXFORD FIELDPATHS SOCIETY

History

On the initiative of a number of people concerned about the increased use of the motor car on the footpaths in the countryside around Oxford, a meeting was held on 26th January 1926 'to form a Society for the preservation of Footpaths, Bridlepaths and Commons in the neighbourhood of Oxford. Unless something is done to protect these, many of them will fall out of use and be forgotten. The ordinary road has more and more become either dangerous or disagreeable for the pedestrian, hence the preservation of the footpaths and bridlepaths is more necessary than ever. The latter are generally safer, quieter and pleasanter than modern roads and bring one into much closer touch with the real country`.

The Society duly came into being, and over the years has worked constantly to protect and improve the network of public rights of way, not only in the countryside immediately around Oxford, but across the whole of the county of Oxfordshire. The Society today faces problems similar to those of 1926, but in many ways much more acute, as a result of the construction of new roads, industrial and housing developments and intensive farming.

What the Society does

Through its Executive Committee elected at the AGM, the Society:

- makes representations to and cooperates with the appropriate local authorities on the maintenance, signposting, and waymarking of rights of way.
- submits claims with documentary evidence for additions to the Definitive Map of Rights of Way.
- considers all proposals for alterations to rights of way, but resisting change unless there is significant public benefit.
- cooperates with other amenity societies on the above matters.
- owns tools which are available to members and other organisations for path clearance work.
- arranges a programme of organised walks which is sent to all members. Walks are normally on Saturdays. The starting point of some walks can be reached by public transport. Dogs are welcome, but should be kept on a lead at all times.

Application for Membership to: David Godfrey, General Secretary, 23 Hawkswell House, Hawkswell Gardens, Oxford OX2 7EX.

Introduction

The D´Arcy Dalton Way, which was created to mark the Oxford Fieldpath Society´s Diamond Jubilee in 1986, was devised by the author to resolve the problem that the existing or projected official or unofficial long-distance paths within Oxfordshire frequently started or finished at points which were difficult to reach by public transport and fanned out from the Chilterns in the southeast of the county to the north and the west where there was no link between them. The idea was therefore to create a link along the western boundary of the county between the Oxford Canal towpath north of Banbury, the Oxfordshire Way, Thames Path and Ridgeway in order to provide long-distance circuits combining part or all of the D´Arcy Dalton Way with parts of two or more of the other long-distance routes, to which access could be taken from some point on the route such as Oxford (on the Thames Path and Oxford Canal towpath) where good public transport links are available. At the same time, however, the fact that the 66-mile-long route in fulfilling this function leads you through some of the remotest and most beautiful countryside in the county including the Redland Hills, Cotswolds, Thames Valley, Vale of the White Horse and Wessex Downs makes it a superb long-distance path in its own right.

The route is described in a north-south direction as the Wessex Downs, which are capped by the Ridgeway and Wayland´s Smithy, first come into view some 30 miles short of your destination and thus provide a focal point for the second half of the Way when walking southwards and the backdrop, which they provide, creates more interesting views when crossing the flatter parts of the Thames Valley and Vale of the White Horse than are available in the other direction.

The name, D´Arcy Dalton Way commemorates the most notable defender of Oxfordshire´s rights of way, Colonel W.P. d´Arcy Dalton (1893 - 1981). D´Arcy, as he was known to his innumerable friends and colleagues, was a founder member of the Oxford Fieldpaths Society in 1926 and its first assistant secretary. Thereafter, for over fifty years he served the Society first as Honorary Secretary, then as Executive Committee member and Chairman and finally as President. He was also for many years chairman of the CPRE Rights of Way Committee, which he was indeed instrumental in establishing. He seems to have walked practically every path in the county, and to have remembered them all, and his unrivalled knowledge, freely shared, has done much to protect Oxfordshire fieldpaths. He cared passionately for rights of way, and wanted everyone to have a chance to enjoy them. It was therefore good that his widow, Mrs. Julia Dalton, readily agreed to the walk being named after him and took the trouble to travel to Sarsden Cross to perform the ceremonial opening of the Way on 27th September 1987.

As the availability of overnight accommodation varies from year to year, it is advisable to contact a local tourist information centre for up-to-date information and bookings. These are as follows:-

Banbury : tel 01295-259855 / fax 01295-270556
Burford : tel 01993-823558 / fax 01993-823590
Cherwell Valley Motorway Service Area (M40 Jct. 10): tel 01869-345888 / fax 01869-345777
Chipping Norton : tel 01608-644379
Faringdon : tel/fax 01367-242191
Northleach : tel 01451-860715
Oxford : tel 01865-726871
Stow-on-the-Wold (Cotswold) : tel 01451-831082 / fax 01451-870083
Wantage : tel 01235-760176
Witney : tel/fax 01993-775802

Both the D´Arcy Dalton Way and the circular walks described here follow public rights of way, use recognised permissive paths or cross public open space. As the majority of paths used cross land used for economic purposes such as agriculture, forestry or the rearing of game, walkers are urged to follow the Country Code at all times (see page 12). Observing these rules helps prevent financial loss to landowners and damage to the environment, as well as the all-too-frequent and sometimes justified bad feeling towards walkers in the countryside.

Details of how to reach the starting points of the circular walks by car and where to park are given in the introductory information to each walk and any convenient railway stations are shown on the accompanying plan. As bus services are liable to frequent change, including information in this book might prove more misleading than helpful and so those wishing to reach the walks by bus are advised to obtain up-to-date information by phoning Oxfordshire County Council´s Public Transport Section on 01865-810405.

While it is hoped that the special maps provided for the D´Arcy Dalton Way and with each circular walk will assist the user to avoid going astray and skeleton details of the surrounding road network are given to enable walkers to vary the route in emergency, it is always advisable to take an Ordnance Survey map with you to enable you to vary the route without using roads or get your bearings if you do become seriously lost. Details of the appropriate maps are given in the introductory information for each section of the Way and each circular walk.

As for other equipment, readers are advised that some mud will normally be encountered particularly in woodland except in the driest weather. However proper walking boots are to be recommended at all times as, even when there are no mud problems, hard ruts or rough surfaces make the protection given by boots to the ankles desirable. In addition, as few Oxfordshire paths are heavily used, overgrowth is prevalent around stiles and hedge gaps particularly in summer. To avoid resultant discomfort, protective clothing is therefore always advisable.

In order to assist in coordinating the plans and the texts, all the numbers of paths used have been shown on the plans and incorporated into the texts. These numbers consist of the official County Council footpath number with prefix letters used to indicate the parish (or in Warwickshire, the district) concerned. It is therefore most helpful to use these when reporting any path problems you may find, together, if possible, with the national grid reference for the precise location of the trouble spot, as, in this way, the problem can be identified on the ground with a minimum of time loss in looking for it. National grid references can, however, only be calculated with the help of Ordnance Survey Landranger, Explorer, Outdoor Leisure or Pathfinder maps and an explanation of how this is done can be found in the Key to all except Pathfinder maps.

The length of time required for any particular section of the Way or circular walk depends on a number of factors such as your personal walking speed, the number of hills, stiles, etc. to be negotiated, whether or not you stop to rest, eat or drink, investigate places of interest etc. and the number of impediments such as mud, crops, overgrowth, ploughing, etc. which you encounter, but generally an average speed of between two and two and a half miles per hour is about right. It is, however, always advisable to allow extra time if you are limited by the daylight or catching a particular bus or train home in order to avoid your walk developing into a race against the clock.

Should you have problems with any of the paths used or find that the description given is no longer correct, the author would be most grateful if you could let him have details (c/o The Book Castle), so that attempts can be made to rectify the problem or the text can be corrected at the next reprint. Nevertheless, the author hopes that you will not encounter any serious problems and have pleasure from following the Way and circular walks.

Distance Table

Height (metres)	Place	Distance miles	km	Cumulative miles	km
120	Wormleighton Reservoir	0.0	0.0	0.0	0.0
145	A423	1.1	1.7	1.1	1.7
160	Farnborough Church	0.6	1.0	1.7	2.7
150	Farnborough/Mollington rd	0.2	0.4	1.9	3.1
165	Warks./Oxon. boundary	0.4	0.6	2.3	3.7
155	Mollington Church	1.0	1.6	3.3	5.3
105	M40 / Oxon/Warks boundary	1.7	2.7	5.0	8.0
160	Shotteswell Green	0.9	1.5	5.9	9.5
165	B4100 (Shotteswell Turn)	0.2	0.4	6.1	9.9
130	Warks/Oxon boundary	0.7	1.1	6.8	11.0
175	Glebe Farm, Horley	0.5	0.8	7.3	11.8
190	Bush Hill	0.8	1.3	8.1	13.1
150	Hornton Green	0.9	1.4	9.0	14.5
180	A422 (Alkerton Turn)	1.3	2.0	10.3	16.5
170	Shenington Church	1.0	1.6	11.3	18.1
180	Yarn Hill Farm	1.2	2.0	12.5	20.1
185	Epwell, 'Chandlers Arms'	1.0	1.7	13.5	21.8
210	B4035 (junction with SG17)	0.9	1.5	14.4	23.3
175	Burdrop, 'Bishop Blaize Inn'	0.8	1.3	15.2	24.6
175	Sibford Ferris road junction	0.2	0.3	15.4	24.9
180	Sibford Grounds Farm	0.7	1.1	16.1	26.0
145	River Stour	0.6	1.0	16.7	27.0
190	Nill Cottages, Hook Norton	1.0	1.6	17.7	28.6
155	Hook Norton, East End	1.1	1.6	18.8	30.2
160	Hook Norton, 'Bell Inn'	0.4	0.6	19.2	30.8
200	South Hill	0.8	1.4	20.0	32.2
220	Unmade unclassified road	1.1	1.7	21.1	33.9
210	Great Rollright Church	0.6	1.0	21.7	34.9
220	Great Rollright crossroads	0.4	0.6	22.1	35.5
215	A3400	1.0	1.7	23.1	37.2
165	Little Rollright hamlet	1.1	1.7	24.2	38.9
145	Salford Green	1.2	1.9	25.4	40.8
145	A44	0.4	0.6	25.8	41.4
145	Glebe Farm, Cornwell	0.7	1.2	26.5	42.6
160	Cornwell road junction	0.8	1.4	27.3	44.0
145	Kingham Hill Farm	0.7	1.1	28.0	45.1
120	Swailsford Bridge Bridleway	0.4	0.7	28.4	45.8
165	Churchill Church (B4450)	1.2	2.0	29.6	47.8

Height (metres)	Place	Distance miles	km	Cumulative miles	km
160	Sarsden Cross	0.7	1.1	30.3	48.9
185	Lord Moreton's Seat	0.9	1.4	31.2	50.3
110	Lyneham crossroads	1.6	2.5	32.8	52.8
110	Oxfordshire Way (Bruern)	1.2	1.9	34.0	54.7
135	Snow Hill	1.0	1.7	35.0	56.4
160	Fifield Church	0.9	1.5	35.9	57.9
175	A424	0.7	1.0	36.6	58.9
155	Tangley	0.5	0.9	37.1	59.8
165	Junction TY1/TY2, Taynton	1.5	2.4	38.6	62.2
185	Miletree Clump (Glos.bdy)	0.5	0.8	39.1	63.0
130	Great Barrington village hall	1.6	2.6	40.7	65.6
125	Little Barrington Church	0.7	1.1	41.4	66.7
160	A40	0.4	0.7	41.8	67.4
140	B4425 (Glos/Oxon bdy)	0.8	1.3	42.6	68.7
120	Westwell War Memorial	0.9	1.4	43.5	70.1
130	Holwell Church	0.8	1.2	44.3	71.3
130	Akeman Street	0.5	0.8	44.8	72.1
95	A361	1.9	3.1	46.7	75.2
85	Filkins, main street	0.8	1.2	47.5	76.4
85	B4477	0.2	0.3	47.7	76.7
80	Broadwell Church	0.9	1.5	48.6	78.2
75	Calcroft Lane	1.4	2.2	50.0	80.4
70	Little Clanfield	1.0	1.7	51.0	82.1
70	Langley Lane	0.7	1.2	51.7	83.3
70	Radcot Bridge (A4095/Thames Path)	0.9	1.5	52.6	84.8
70	Eaton Hastings Church	1.7	2.8	54.3	87.6
85	A417 (Buscot Park Lodge)	1.4	2.2	55.7	89.8
85	Oldfield Farm	0.6	0.9	56.3	90.7
95	Brimstone Farm	0.5	0.8	56.8	91.5
130	B4019 (junction with CO13)	1.2	2.0	58.0	93.5
105	Ashen Copse Farm	0.7	1.1	58.7	94.6
105	A420	1.4	2.2	60.1	96.8
95	Longcot Church (B4508)	1.4	2.2	61.5	99.0
90	Claypit Lane	1.4	2.3	62.9	101.3
90	Marsh Way	0.3	0.5	63.2	101.8
105	Knighton	1.0	1.6	64.2	103.4
110	Compton Beauchamp Church	0.3	0.5	64.5	103.9
150	B4507	1.0	1.5	65.5	105.4
210	Ridgeway Path (jct. AS19)	0.7	1.1	66.2	106.5
215	Wayland's Smithy	0.2	0.4	66.4	106.9

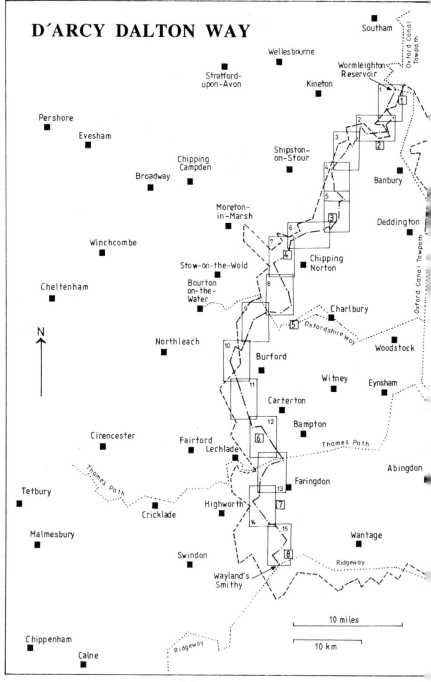

D'ARCY DALTON WAY

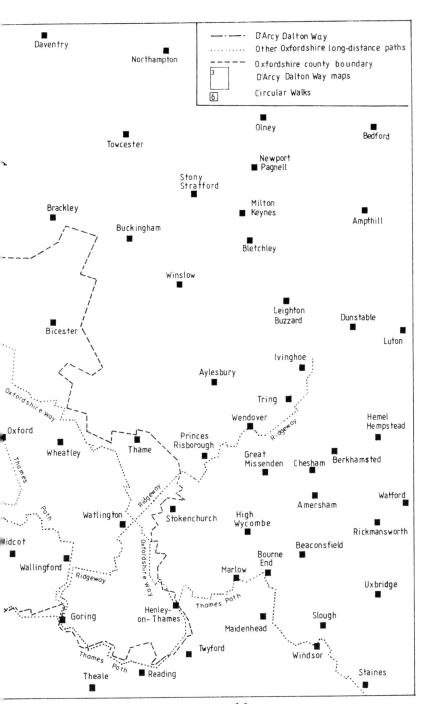

	D'Arcy Dalton Way
	Other Oxfordshire long-distance paths
	Oxfordshire county boundary
	D'Arcy Dalton Way maps
	Circular Walks

Daventry

Northampton

Olney

Bedford

Towcester

Newport Pagnell

Stony Stratford

Brackley

Milton Keynes

Ampthill

Buckingham

Bletchley

Winslow

Leighton Buzzard

Dunstable

Luton

Bicester

Ivinghoe

Aylesbury

Tring

Wendover

Hemel Hempstead

Oxfordshire Way

Oxford

Princes Risborough

Ridgeway

Wheatley

Thame

Great Missenden

Chesham

Berkhamsted

Thames

Watford

Ridgeway

Amersham

Watlington

Stokenchurch

High Wycombe

Rickmansworth

Path

Oxfordshire way

idcot

Beaconsfield

Wallingford

Ridgeway

Bourne End

Marlow

Uxbridge

Thames Path

Goring

Henley- on- Thames

Slough

Maidenhead

Thames

Path

Twyford

Windsor

Staines

Theale

Reading

Country Code

- Guard against all risk of fire

- Fasten all gates

- Keep dogs under proper control

- Keep to the paths across farmland

- Avoid damaging fences, hedges and walls

- Leave no litter - take it home

- Safeguard water supplies

- Protect wild life, wild plants and trees

- Go carefully on country roads on the right-hand side facing oncoming traffic

- Respect the life of the countryside

GUIDE TO THE D'ARCY DALTON WAY

Access to Wormleighton Reservoir

Access to or from Wormleighton Reservoir by public transport is difficult as there is no longer a railway station in the area and bus services are highly infrequent. The simplest way to get to or from the starting point of the D'Arcy Dalton Way is therefore to travel to Banbury which has regular bus and train services and walk to Wormleighton Reservoir by way of the Oxford Canal towpath which passes close to both bus and railway station. Although this is a 9-mile walk, by definition the route is flat and easy and much of it is very pleasant.

Wormleighton Reservoir - Farnborough (Map 1)

OS Maps
Landranger Sheet 151
Explorer Sheet 206
Pathfinder Sheet 999 (SP45/55)

Wormleighton Reservoir on the edge of Warwickshire, from the banks of which the D'Arcy Dalton Way starts, is one of three reservoirs in three different counties feeding water to the summit of the nearby Oxford Canal. This canal, first planned in 1768 to link the River Thames to waterways in the Midlands and provide a more reliable way to deliver goods, in particular coal, to Banbury, Oxford and the upper Thames Valley than the Thames with its frequent tendency to flood, opened north of Banbury in 1778 and reached Oxford and the Thames in 1790. Designed by the renowned canal builder James Brindley, the Oxford Canal was initially a great success, more than halving the price of coal in Banbury overnight, but the completion of the Grand Junction Canal, which provided a more direct route from the Midlands to London, and the building of the railways reduced its economic importance and today it only carries pleasure boats.

13

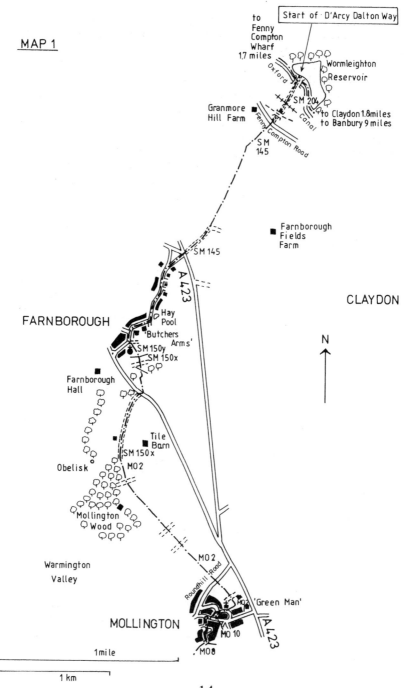

MAP 1

Start of D'Arcy Dalton Way

to Fenny Compton Wharf 1.7 miles

Oxford Canal

Wormleighton Reservoir

SM 204

Granmore Hill Farm

Fenny Compton Road

to Claydon 1.8 miles
to Banbury 9 miles

SM 145

Farnborough Fields Farm

SM 145

A 423

CLAYDON

N

FARNBOROUGH

Hay Pool

'Butchers Arms'

SM 150y
SM 150x

Farnborough Hall

Tile Barn

SM 150x

Obelisk

MO 2

Mollington Wood

Warmington Valley

MO 2

Roundhill Road

'Green Man'

MOLLINGTON

MO 10

A 423

MO 8

1 mile

1 km

14

Starting from the banks of Wormleighton Reservoir by the end of bridge no.139 over the Oxford Canal, take bridleway SM204 over this bridge and through gates, then follow a left-hand hedge to a gated level-crossing over the Oxford & Birmingham Railway built in 1852. Cross this by way of its white-painted bridgegates, then continue beside the left-hand hedge through another gate and an archway (bearing the former East & West Junction Railway from Bedford to Stratford-upon-Avon, built in the 1860s and closed, like so many other cross-country links, 100 years later by Dr. Beeching) to reach a bridlegate onto Fenny Compton Road.

Here take bridleway SM145 through a gate opposite bearing slightly right across a first field to a gate. Now go straight on across a second field towards two gates right of a hedge corner. Do **not** go through these but instead bear left through a second pair of gates into a third field and bear half right across the field to gates in its far corner where Farnborough comes into view ahead and there are views towards Wormleighton behind you. Now go straight on across the next field towards Farnborough to a gate where you follow a right-hand fence straight on to join a farm road at a bend. Here take this farm road with views to your left towards Claydon, Oxfordshire's most northerly village, climbing gently to reach the A423, Banbury to Coventry road, on the edge of Farnborough.

Farnborough - Mollington (Map 1)

OS Maps
Landranger Sheet 151
Explorer Sheet 206
Pathfinder Sheets 999 (SP45/55) & 1022 (SP44/54)

Farnborough (Warks.), not to be confused with its Hampshire namesake of airshow fame, is a quiet village in a ridgetop hollow off the A423 with picturesque ironstone cottages, some thatched. The village is best-known for Farnborough Hall, an eighteenth-century classical house owned by the National Trust and can also boast a twelfth-century church largely rebuilt in the fourteenth century with its distinctive spire silhouetted against the sky.

Cross the main road carefully and take the Farnborough and Avon Dassett road straight on uphill into the village with fine views across three counties behind you, then continue over the hill into the next valley, bearing right by the village hall and passing the ´Butcher´s Arms`. Now go round a left-hand bend and fork left onto path SM150y with a safety rail to your right, crossing a gravel drive, passing through a squeeze-stile between ironstone cottages and taking a walled path to a lychgate into Farnborough Churchyard. Here follow a left-hand wall straight on, passing left of the fine ironstone church to reach a lychgate into a field. Now take bridleway SM150x straight on downhill until a fence bars your way ahead then turn right beside this fence to its corner where you bear left, gradually diverging from the fence with views of the village behind you to cross a stile right of several gates onto the Mollington road.

Cross this and bear slightly right through two gates into Farnborough Park. Now take a faintly-perceptible grass track bearing slightly left across this typical eighteenth-century park, passing left of an oak tree on the skyline and a clump of oaks shading an old shed to reach a bridlegate at the near corner of Mollington Wood, shortly before which there are views to your right of an obelisk and the Warmington valley. Go through this bridlegate entering Oxfordshire and take path MO2 along the outside edge of the wood to another bridlegate onto a farm road. Cross this and go straight on, passing right of an oak tree then bearing slightly left past a wooden pylon to cross a farm track and reach a hedge gap under an oak tree at the right-hand end of a small coniferous plantation. Now go straight on across the next field to cross another farm track and step over hurdles, then follow a left-hand fence and sporadic hedge with fine views to your right across the Warmington valley towards Shotteswell. At the far side of the field cross a stile by a gate, Roundhill Road and another stile and follow a right-hand fence through two fields to a gate and stile onto a macadam drive. Go straight on across this and a lawn into a fenced path leading to a kissing-gate into Mollington Churchyard. Now follow the gravel churchyard path passing left of the church to a gate, then continue along the gravel path to join Church Lane in Mollington.

Mollington - Shotteswell (Map 2)

OS Maps
Landranger Sheet 151
Explorer Sheet 206
Pathfinder Sheet 1022 (SP44/54)

Mollington, a hillside village dropping from the ridge bearing the A423 into the Warmington valley, is another village of fine ironstone cottages which was once split between Oxfordshire and Warwickshire. Its fourteenth-century church with a fifteenth-century tower obviously replaced an earlier building as its font dates from the time of the Normans.

At a right-hand bend in Church Lane turn left onto path MO10 down an old green lane known as Blacksmiths Lane to Main Street. Here turn right then left into Chestnut Road. At the bottom turn right, then left, then right again to reach Mollington Village Hall. Now take fenced path MO8 crossing a stile left of the hall and continuing past the school playing field to a stile into a field. Here turn right and follow a right-hand hedge round two sides of the field then turn right through a gate and right again to follow a right-hand hedge through two fields for nearly half a mile with fine views towards Shotteswell ahead to reach the M40 fence. Now turn left and follow this fence for two-thirds of a mile through four fields (on path CP7 as from the second field) to reach a footbridge over the motorway. Here bear left and follow the fence surrounding the bridge to reach the access to the bridge then turn sharp right onto path CP1 crossing the motorway bridge and continuing along a fenced path to cross a footbridge over the Avon (a tributary of the Cherwell after which the nearby Warwickshire village of Avon Dassett is named and not the river at Stratford-upon-Avon).
Now in Warwickshire again with fine views ahead towards Shotteswell, take path SM162 turning sharp right and following the Avon into a field corner. Here cross a footbridge and follow the Avon straight on parallel to the M40 to the far side of the next field, then turn left and follow a right-hand hedge until you reach a stile in it. Cross this and follow a left-hand hedge straight on for nearly half a mile through three fields to reach the concrete drive to Shotteswell Sewage Works. Now bear half left towards the church to reach a gate into a green lane by a wooden pylon and follow the lane uphill to reach Bakehouse Lane in Shotteswell.

Shotteswell - Hornton (Map 2)

OS Maps
Landranger Sheet 151
Explorer Sheet 206
Pathfinder Sheets 1021 (SP24/34) & 1022 (SP44/54)

The Warwickshire hillside village of Shotteswell, surrounded on three sides by Oxfordshire, is another picturesque ironstone village with a fine seventeenth-century manor house and other large houses. It also can boast a prominent twelfth-century church with a thirteenth-century tower which was much altered in the fourteenth century.

Turn left into Bakehouse Lane then immediately turn right and take Middle Lane uphill through Shotteswell. Near the top of the hill bear right to a small green then left onto the road signposted to Banbury and Warwick and follow it for a quarter mile to the B4100 (formerly part of the A41 London-Birmingham trunk road).

Turn right onto this road towards Warmington and Gaydon, then, after about 100 yards, turn left crossing the main road and a stile opposite onto path SM202. In the field bear slightly right to keep right of a grassy bank then half left passing left of a barn and following a powerline to a gate and stile in the top corner of the field. Here follow a right-hand hedge for about 80 yards to a gate and stile in it, then turn right over the stile and bear half left across a field heading for Horley Fields Farm, the right-hand and smaller of two farms on the next ridge, soon with fine views across the Sor Brook valley ahead and towards Edge Hill to your right, scene in 1642 of the first major battle of the Civil War, to cross a stile in the far corner of the field. Now bear half left across the next field, aiming slightly right of Horley Fields Farm to cross a footbridge just right of the far corner of the field. Here the path should bear half left across the corner of the next field to cross Sor Brook into Oxfordshire and then take path HL18 beside a left-hand hedge to a gap into the next field, but currently it is necessary to turn left and follow the left-hand hedge to a footbridge and stile over Sor Brook, then continue across the next field to a footbridge and stiles leading you back onto the correct route of path HL18. Now go straight on across the next field to the corner of a fence by some hawthorn bushes. Here bear half right briefly joining the fence, then, where the fence bears right again, leave it and go straight on uphill to a gate in a corner of the field. Now bear half left onto a macadam

MAP 2

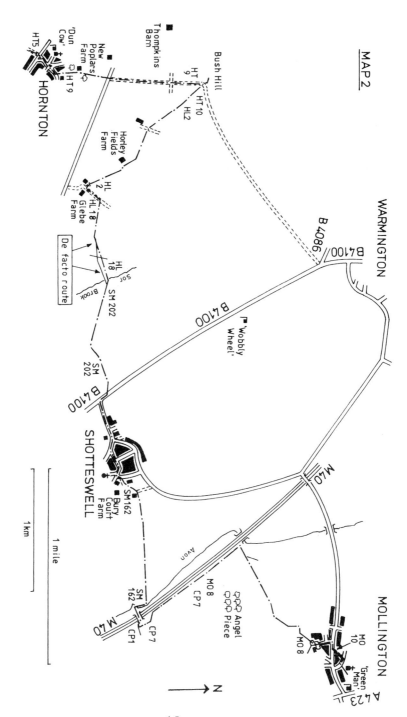

HT5

'Dun
Cow'

HORNTON

New
Poplars
Farm

HT 9

Thompkins
Barn

HT
9

Bush Hill

HT 10

HL2

Horley
Fields
Farm

HL
2

HL 18

Glebe
Farm

De facto route

HL
18

S of
Brook

SM 202

SM
202

WARMINGTON

B 4086

B4100

B4100

'Wobbly
Wheel'

B4100

SHOTTESWELL

SM162

Bury
Court
Farm

M40

Avon

SM
162

CP1

CP 7

M40

M08

CP7

'Angel
Piece'

M08

MOLLINGTON

MO
10

'Green
Man'

A423

1km

1 mile

N

19

farm road and follow it uphill to Glebe Farm.

At the farm turn right between a barn and a diesel tank onto path HL2 passing right of the barn and following a rough track. Where this turns left through a hedge gap, go straight on over a stile and follow a left-hand hedge with fine views to your right. About 100 yards short of the far end of the field at a slight kink in the hedge by Horley Fields Farm to your left, cross a stile and follow the other side of the hedge to a field corner. Here cross a stile and turn left following a left-hand hedge to a gap in the next hedge, then cross a track and bear half right across the next field with fine views to your right to reach a gap just left of the far corner. Go through this and take path HT10 straight on across the next field to a stile in the far hedge at Bush Hill where superb panoramic views open out across the Sor Brook valley towards Edge Hill ahead and Shotteswell on the hilltop to your right.

Here turn left onto fenced cart-track HT9 and follow it straight on for half a mile, soon with a fine view to your left towards Northamptonshire, ignoring a crossing track leading to a farm to your right. On reaching the Horley-Upton road, cross it and take path HT9 straight on over a stile following a left-hand fence to cross a second stile. Here bear slightly right across the next field to pass just right of two sycamore trees and cross a stile behind them. Now follow a right-hand hedge downhill going through a gate, then pass right of a stone wall and a cottage and go through its gates and down its drive to reach a road in Hornton called Eastgate.

Hornton - Shenington (Map 3)

OS Maps
Landranger Sheet 151
Explorer Sheet 206
Pathfinder Sheet 1021 (SP24/34)

Hornton, with its attractive village green in a sheltered valley, is appropriately another village of fine ironstone cottages, as it is renowned for its building stone used in the construction of Liverpool Cathedral as well as many of the older houses in Banbury. Though still known as Hornton stone, it is no longer quarried in the village but instead at nearby Edge Hill, just over the Warwickshire border. In addition, the village can also boast a twelfth-century church noted for its late fourteenth-century wall-painting of the Last Judgement over its chancel arch.

Take Eastgate downhill to The Green. At its bottom end fork right, passing right of a thatched cottage with a fine wisteria in front of you and taking bridleway HT5 straight on uphill. On entering a deep sunken way, ignore a branching path to your left, then where the sunken way regains ground level, there is a fine view across Hornton over a gate to your right. Here bear left and take a fenced grassy track with wide views to your left, soon passing between ironstone quarries. (NB At the time of writing (1998), bridleway HT5 has been temporarily diverted around the quarries, but it is due to be restored to its original route before publication). Beyond the quarries ignore a branching track to your left and take the fenced track straight on to Hornton Grounds Farm. Here go straight on across the farmyard to pass between the last barn and a set of gates then bear slightly left following a track beside a right-hand fence to reach a bend in the macadam farm drive. Take this drive straight on for over a quarter mile rounding a right-hand bend then, where the drive forks, take bridleway SA19 straight on to a gate by a water-tower leading to the A422 Banbury - Stratford-upon-Avon road.

Turn right onto this road ignoring the entrance to Hornton Grounds Quarry to your right, then at a road junction turn left onto a road signposted ´Recycling & Waste Centre`. Some 80 yards beyond a cottage at the road junction turn right over a stile onto path SA8 bearing half left across a field to cross a concealed stile in the hedge left of the far corner. Now bear half right across a corner of the next field to cross another concealed stile in the right-hand hedge where Shenington comes into view ahead backed by Yarn Hill, Epwell Hill and Rough Hill with Shenlow Hill further to the right. Here bear half left across the next field heading just right of a copse known as The Plantation and a tall ash tree in the next hedge to cross a rustic stile, then bear half left again downhill, passing right of a horse-jump to reach a gate on a grassy track right of the right-hand corner of the copse. Now follow this track to pass through another gate, then leave the track and go straight on past a spring where you bear slightly right briefly glimpsing Alkerton's hillside twelfth-century church with a thirteenth-century tower to your left. In the bottom corner of the field cross a stile and follow a left-hand hedge through a marshy area to cross a series of stiles and footbridges leading to a meadow. Now take path SA14 bearing slightly right across the meadow to pass between a row of poplars and a hedge corner, then follow the hedge uphill to a stile in the field corner leading in a few yards to the village street in Shenington.

MAP 3

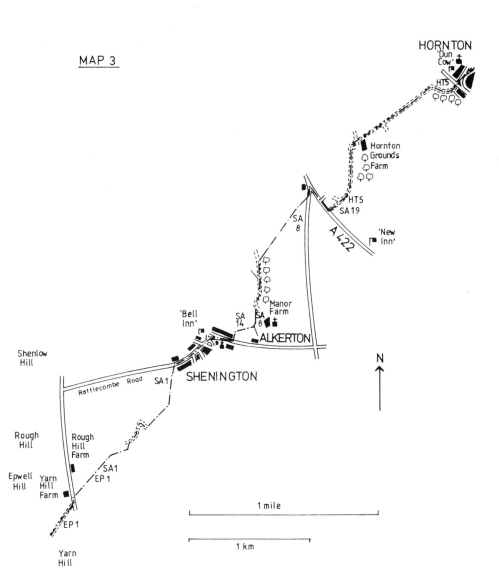

Shenington - Yarn Hill Farm (Map 3)

OS Maps
Landranger Sheet 151
Explorer Sheet 206
Pathfinder Sheet 1021 (SP24/34)

Shenington, once a detached enclave of Gloucestershire, with its picturesque hilltop green and stone cottages, would be the epitome of a Gloucestershire Cotswold village, were it not for the colour of the stone which firmly places it in the Redlands. A vital contribution to its beauty is made by its twelfth-century church with a fifteenth-century embattled tower, which is notable for a fine Norman chancel arch which is now part of its north wall.

Turn right into the village street and follow it uphill past the church to the green where the ˋBell Innˋ is to your right. Now keep straight on to the far end of the village. Where the left-hand houses end, ignore a gate to your left and fork left over a concealed rail-stile onto path SA1 following a left-hand fence downhill to cross a footbridge. Now bear slightly left across the next field to its top left-hand corner. Here go through the right-hand of two gates and follow a left-hand hedge with Epwell Hill and Rough Hill coming into view ahead and Shenlow Hill to your right. At the far end of this field go through a hunting-gate and bear half right following a terraced track downhill, then, near the bottom, bear left to cross a gated culvert. In the next field bear slightly left following a grassy track round the contours of the hill to cross a stile by a gate. Here bear slightly left passing left of a clump of bushes concealing a spring then following a left-hand hedge to a footbridge. Cross this and after a few yards turn left over a stile and bear half right heading just left of a clump of ash trees on the skyline to cross a stile then continue downhill to cross a footbridge and stile in the field corner. Now take path EP1 bearing half right across a field passing just left of a wooden electricity pylon with close-up views of (from left to right) Yarn Hill, Epwell Hill and Rough Hill opening out ahead, to reach a stile onto a road opposite the left-hand end of Yarn Hill Farm.

Yarn Hill Farm - Epwell (Map 4)

OS Maps
Landranger Sheet 151
Explorer Sheet 206
Pathfinder Sheet 1021 (SP24/34)

Turn left onto this road, then, after 30 yards, turn right through a
gate (still on path EP1) and take a farm track beside a right-hand
hedge to a gate at the far side of the field. Now follow the right-
hand hedge straight on for a further third of a mile through a large
field and two paddocks passing Yarn Hill to your left and with
Epwell coming into view ahead. In the second paddock ignore a
stile of a crossing path in the right-hand hedge, then at the far side
of the paddock cross a stile and bear half left towards an ironstone
cottage crossing a footbridge then continuing across a lawn to pass
right of a leylandii and follow the cottage drive to a gate leading to
Birds Lane in Epwell.

Epwell - Burdrop (Map 4)

OS Maps
Landranger Sheet 151
Explorer Sheets 191 & 206
Pathfinder Sheets 1021 (SP24/34) & 1044 (SP23/33)

**Epwell, another remote village on the Warwickshire border with
picturesque ironstone cottages, some of which are thatched, like
its equally remote neighbours Shutford and the Sibfords, was
formerly a chapelry of Swalcliffe (pronounced ´Swaycliff´) which
is noted for its fine church, one of the few in the county of Saxon
origin, while Epwell´s own tiny church dates from the thirteenth
century.**

Turn right onto the road, passing a number of attractive cottages, some thatched, and ignoring two branching paths to your right, then having rounded a left-hand bend, at a road junction by the church turn right. At the far end of the churchyard turn left onto path EP6 following a sunken way gently uphill. On emerging into a field, bear half right across it heading for a twin-poled wooden pylon to reach a hedge gap at the far corner of the field where you go straight on through the ´Chandlers Arms` car park to reach another road.

Turn left onto it passing the pub, then at a small green fork right onto a stony drive, turning right again at a crossways onto bridleway EP11 which leaves the green and enters a field by way of a gate right of ´The Willows`. Now bear left following a left-hand fence then a hedge passing left of a fenced pond to reach a corner of the field. Here go through the right-hand of two gates then take path SG17 bearing half right across the next field with fine views to your left of Barton Hill and Madmarston Hill, keeping right of a powerline to go through gates in the top hedge onto bridleway SG15. Turn right onto this, then, after 20 yards by the corner of a fence, take the continuation of path SG17 bearing half left across a field to cross a concealed stile in the far hedge. Now bear slightly left heading for a wooden pylon in a hedge right of some ruined farm buildings where you join the hedge and follow it to a bend in a farm track by the buildings where there are superb views across North Oxfordshire to your left with (from left to right) Epwell Hill, Yarn Hill, Barton Hill and Madmarston Hill in the foreground. Here turn right onto the track, then just past the ruined buildings turn left between them and a right-hand hedge. Just past the buildings ignore a gate to your right and follow the right-hand hedge straight on to a hedge gap in the field corner, then bear slightly right across the next field to cross a stile just left of its far right-hand corner. Now bear slightly right across the next field then continue across one more field to a gate in the far corner leading to the B4035.

Turn left onto this road and follow it for over 300 yards ignoring the first signposted path to your right, then turn right through a gate onto path SG13 following a left-hand hedge for a quarter mile looking out for a stile in it. Turn left over this stile and bear half right across a large field heading towards a modern house in Burdrop to reach a gate in the far corner of the field. Go through this and follow a right-hand fence to reach a stile at the corner of a hedge leading in a few yards to a bend in Hawk´s Lane at Burdrop.

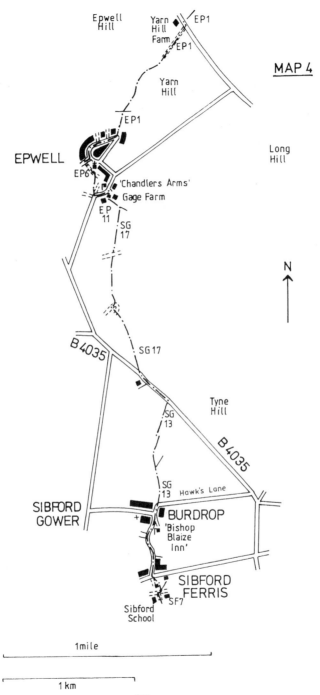

Burdrop - Sibford Ferris (Map 4)

OS Maps
Landranger Sheet 151
Explorer Sheet 191
Pathfinder Sheet 1044 (SP23/33)

Burdrop, a hillside hamlet of Sibford Gower parish, which like Epwell was once attached to Swalcliffe, has now virtually become joined to Sibford Gower and is unusually the site of Sibford Gower´s parish church, only built by H.J. Underwood in 1840. Despite their small size each village still has its own pub and a scattering of attractive ironstone cottages.

Now turn right into Hawk´s Lane, then at a T-junction fork left onto the Sibford Ferris road and follow it downhill, ignoring side turnings to your left and passing the ´Bishop Blaize Inn`. Having crossed a bridge over a stream in the valley bottom, continue uphill to a T-junction in Sibford Ferris.

Sibford Ferris - Hook Norton (Map 5)

OS Maps
Landranger Sheet 151
Explorer Sheet 191
Pathfinder Sheet 1044 (SP23/33)

The ridgetop village of Sibford Ferris is unusual in not having its own parish church and since 1842 it has been an important centre for Oxfordshire Quakers as in that year the Society of Friends converted the village´s much remodelled seventeenth-century manor house into the nucleus of the modern Sibford School, one of only nine Quaker schools in England.

At the T-junction in Sibford Ferris take path SF7 straight on up a flight of stone steps and over stone and wooden stiles left of the entrance to Sibford School. Now follow a right-hand fence straight on uphill passing a stone shed and a house to your right to reach a kissing-gate leading to a junction of drives. Here go straight on over a stile by a gate and follow a macadam drive through the grounds of Sibford School. On nearing the Sports Hall, just past the end of a hedge to your left, turn left over a stile and take a fenced path to another stile where you turn right and walk between a right-hand fence and young trees to reach a hedge. Here turn left onto a fenced path to cross a stile in the hedge then bear slightly left across a field aiming just left of a stone shed ahead to reach the bottom corner of the field. Now go straight on through a gap then turn left onto a farm road with fine views to your right across the upper reaches of the Stour valley towards Whichford Hill and the Cotswolds (the Stour being the one Oxfordshire river which flows northwestwards into Warwickshire past Shipston-on-Stour to enter the Avon near Stratford-upon-Avon and thence the River Severn).

After 300 yards you then enter a hedged lane leading to Sibford Grounds Farm. At the farm pass left of a lawn then bear right then left along a track between the buildings which also bears right then left, ignoring a gate to your right and continuing to gates into a field. Bear half right across the field corner then take a sunken way beside a right-hand hedge to a gate. Here bear slightly right across the next field to join its right-hand hedge by an ash tree and follow it downhill (now on bridleway SF9) to a gate into a strip of woodland in Hill Bottom. Now take the enclosed bridleway straight on through the wood for 200 yards with a hedge to your right and a slight ravine to your left with a stream in the bottom. On passing through an old gate, you leave the mature woodland and continue along its outside edge with a young plantation to your right until you reach the corner of a field. Here turn left through a hedge gap reentering the wood, stepping over a small stream and taking bridleway SC10 straight on through a wood known as Swalcliffe Common for a quarter mile to reach a farm road (bridleway SC9).

Turn right onto this, crossing a culvert over the incipient River Stour, then leave the farm road and take bridleway HN19 bearing half right across the field towards the right-hand end of a line of poplars right of Lower Nill Farm to reach a gap in the far hedge. Go through this and bear slightly right across the next field with fine views along the Stour valley ahead and to your right towards Sibford Ferris on its hilltop, heading just left of a distant barn and a tall ash tree to reach a gap at the corner of a hedge. Turn left through this and follow the left-hand hedge gently uphill. On reaching a farm road, turn left onto it, then immediately right onto a macadam farm road and follow it gently uphill for over a third of a mile, ignoring a branching farm road to your left, to reach a public road on the ridge top by Nill Cottages where a quaintly-named rural pub called 'The Gate Hangs High' is half a mile to your right.

Cross this road and a stile opposite onto path HN19 with a superb view across Hook Norton opening out in front of you, then bear slightly right, aiming just right of Hook Norton Church, crossing a slight rise then dropping to a hedge gap left of a tall ash tree. Here cross a stile and bear half right across the next field, crossing a fenceline just right of the second large hawthorn bush in the field beyond, then go through a hedge gap descending the steep face of an old ironstone quarry and bear slightly left across the next field to a gate in a fenceline ahead. (NB If there is no stile in the correct position in the first fenceline, turn left and follow the fence to cross an off-line stile in it, then follow a left-hand hedge to descend the old quarry face and bear half right across the next field to a gate where you rejoin the correct path line). Go through this gate and keep straight on across two fields heading for the near end of a tree-belt ahead crossing a stile in the first fenceline and eventually dropping to cross a stile by a gate and a footbridge at the left-hand end of a concealed lake created in part of the old ironstone quarry.

Now continue past a seat and through an area of scrub to a stile in a field corner then follow the left-hand tree-belt straight on. On passing a redundant stile, keep right at a fork and continue to follow the edge of the tree-belt at first. After 50 yards bear half right across the field to a kissing-gate into a belt of scrub. Go through this and take a fenced path through the scrub, soon crossing two residential roads on the edge of Hook Norton and continuing along a gravel path to reach a third near a T-junction. Cross this road and join the main road known as East End, then, at a left-hand bend, turn right onto path HN35 along a gravel drive. Where the drive turns left into private land, take an enclosed path straight on, then, where the path becomes macadamed, keep left at a fork, soon crossing a residential road. At a further fork go left to reach the main village street where you turn right and take Chapel Street becoming High Street to reach the ´Bell Inn` in the village centre.

Hook Norton - South Hill (Map 5)

OS Maps
Landranger Sheet 151
Explorer Sheet 191
Pathfinder Sheet 1044 (SP23/33)

Hook Norton, locally called ´Hookey`, the last ironstone village and largest village on the D´Arcy Dalton Way, is probably best known today for its brewery, one of the smallest in the country which is passed on Circular Walk No.3. Indeed, as recently as 1945, Hook Norton was a hive of industry with, in addition to the brewery, the Brymbo Ironworks, active ironstone quarries and the Banbury-Cheltenham railway built in 1887 crossing the valley on an 80-foot high viaduct. However today the ironworks and railway have closed and the pillars of the viaduct and quarry faces are rapidly disappearing beneath rampant tree cover, so that this large Redland village in its quiet valley with a wealth of fine stone cottages dominated by the impressive Perpendicular tower of its originally Norman church, when seen from the surrounding hills, appears to have descended into an enchanted slumber.

By the ´Bell Inn` turn left down Bell Hill and at the bottom fork right by a postbox into Burycroft Road climbing to a T-junction. Here turn right into Croft´s Lane and where its left-hand houses end, turn left through a gate onto path HN1. (NB It is currently not possible to walk the definitive line of this path due to obstructions and so the de facto line is described. If you find a different line is waymarked, it would be advisable to follow it as it probably means that the path has been restored to its definitive line.) Bear slightly left to go through a second gate then half right across a field to a gate left of an electricity pole. Go through this and straight on across the next field to cross two rail-stiles, then continue across a further field to a gate and rail-stile leading into a green lane. Turn left down this lane to cross a stile by a gate and farm-bridge in the valley bottom then bear slightly right up the next field to go through a gap left of a tall ash tree. Now bear half right to cross rails by a gate left of a clump of ash trees then bear half right across a further field, where there are fine views over Hook Norton behind you, to reach a hedge gap at the right-hand end of a line of trees leading to the road at South Hill.

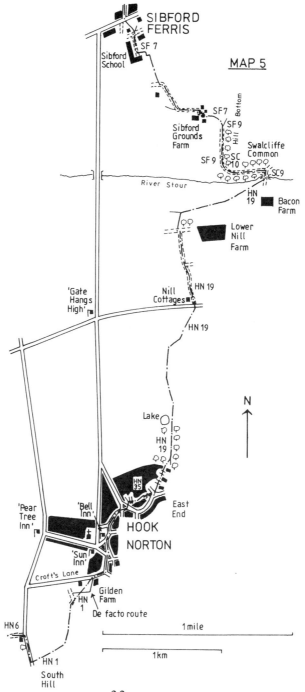

SIBFORD FERRIS

MAP 5

SF 7

Sibford School

SF 7

SF 7 Bottom

Sibford Grounds Farm

SF 9 Hill

SF 9

SC 10

Swalcliffe Common

SF 9

SC 9

River Stour

HN 19

Bacon Farm

Lower Nill Farm

'Gate Hangs High'

Nill Cottages

HN 19

HN 19

N

Lake

HN 19

HN 35

'Pear Tree Inn'

'Bell Inn'

East End

HOOK NORTON

'Sun Inn'

Croft's Lane

Gilden Farm

HN 1

De facto route

HN 6

1 mile

1 km

HN 1

South Hill

33

South Hill - Great Rollright (Map 6)

OS Maps
Landranger Sheet 151
Explorer Sheet 191
Pathfinder Sheet 1044 (SP23/33)

Turn right onto this road and follow it gently downhill. After about 250 yards, at the far end of a row of conifers to your left, turn left onto path HN6, the drive to Fanville Farm, and follow it straight on passing a fine modern timbered house to your left and ignoring all branching tracks and drives. At the far side of the farm go through a gate and take path HN5 straight on, disregarding all gates and branching tracks to left and right and eventually emerging into a left-hand field. Here follow a shallow sunken way straight on by the right-hand hedge, soon becoming enclosed by a left-hand hedge. On reemerging into the field, the sunken way soon peters out. Where the right-hand hedge bears away to the right, leave it and go straight on across the field to a gap in the next hedge, then bear slightly left across the field beyond with fine views behind you towards the Sibfords to reach a hedge gap just right of a stunted oak tree on the skyline, the highest point on the D´Arcy Dalton Way at approximately 221 metres or 725 feet above sea level.

Go through this gap crossing a grassy track then take path RR1 bearing half right across the next field heading just right of a tall sycamore tree in a distant hedge to cross an unclassified road and stone stile in a stone wall. Now bear slightly right across a further field to a gap in a stone wall by a clump of bushes. Here bear half right across a corner of the next field to a hedge gap by the tall sycamore tree where Great Rollright Church comes into view ahead. Now bear slightly right across a further field heading towards a modern barn at Church End Farm right of the church to a rail-stile in the next hedge. Cross this and bear slightly left downhill to cross a footbridge in the valley bottom then bear half left uphill, heading for the church when it comes into view, to cross a stile in the top corner of the field leading to a road. Cross the road and go through a gate opposite into Great Rollright Churchyard then bear half left across the churchyard passing left of the church to reach the lychgate leading to a road known as Church End.

Great Rollright - Little Rollright (Map 6)

OS Maps
Landranger Sheet 151
Outdoor Leisure Sheet 45 & Explorer Sheet 191
Pathfinder Sheet 1044 (SP23/33)

Great Rollright, as immediately becomes obvious on seeing its church, is the first Cotswold limestone village on the D´Arcy Dalton Way. This twelfth-century church with a fifteenth-century tower, though ancient in itself, however, in no way, marks the foundation of the village as Great Rollright is mentioned in the Domesday Book of 1086 and its location on a road thought to be the most ancient in Britain, possibly dating back to the Stone Age, suggests that habitation of this site may go back a long way further. However the many tourists who visit the village in search of the Rollright Stones do so in vain as they are situated nearly 2 miles to the west near Little Rollright on the other side of the A3400 Oxford - Stratford-upon-Avon main road.

Take Church End soon bearing right, then at a road junction go straight on. Now at a right-hand bend fork left through a kissing-gate onto path RR13 heading for a gap in the houses at the far corner of the field. About halfway across the field fork right onto path RR12 crossing a stile at the corner of a hedge then pass right of some garages to join a residential road onto which you turn right then left to reach a T-junction. Here turn right, then at a crossroads turn left onto the Long Compton and Little Rollright road and follow it for a third of a mile. Having passed through a dip, at a slight right-hand bend fork left through gates onto path RR7 (NB if the gates are padlocked, use a gap in the hedge to their left) and follow a short green lane to enter a field where a fine view opens out ahead towards the distant Evenlode valley. Now follow a grassy track beside a right-hand hedge to the far end of the field, then go straight on through a hedge gap and bear slightly left along a grass baulk separating two arable fields, now with views across Warwickshire towards Brailes Hill to your right. On reaching the left-hand corner of a copse, follow its outside edge straight on into a field corner then bear half right into the copse, soon descending some steep steps to reach the busy A3400 Oxford - Stratford-upon-Avon main road.

Turn right along this road then after 20 yards turn sharp left crossing the road and taking the continuation of path RR7 up a

35

sunken way through a tree belt. On nearing a field ahead, turn right through a hedge gap into a field and follow its left-hand hedge. At the far side of the field go straight on through a hedge gap and follow a right-hand hedge, now with fine views to your left towards the outskirts of Chipping Norton and the distant Evenlode valley beyond, eventually crossing a stile onto a farm road. Now continue across two rail-stiles opposite and bear slightly right across the next field to cross two further stiles at the right-hand end of a belt of tall trees, then go through a hedge gap with the Rollright Stones coming into view to your right and fine views opening out down the valley ahead towards Salford and the distant Evenlode valley and to your left towards the outskirts of Chipping Norton on a hill-side.

The Rollright Stones, which are variously believed to be of Neo-lithic or Bronze Age origin and to date from sometime between 2000 B.C. and 1500 B.C., can be divided into three groups: the Whispering Knights, the remains of an ancient burial chamber, near the right-hand hedge of the field; the King´s Men, a circle of 77 stones of various sizes, in the far corner of the field and the King´s Stone, a single eight-foot-high stone on a low mound on the other side of the ridgetop road in Warwickshire. The names would seem to have little to do with the real origin of the stones but rather derive from a local legend that an ancient king, who was attempting to conquer England and was leading his army towards the crest of the Cotswold escarpment, was stopped by a witch who turned them to stone and herself into an elderbush; the King´s Stone being the king, the King´s Men being his army and the Whispering Knights lagging behind and plotting against him. There is no public access to the Whispering Knights which can, indeed, best be seen from where you are on path RR7, while access to the King´s Stone and King´s Men is only available from the ridgetop road. If wishing to take a closer look at them, you should therefore continue along the D´Arcy Dalton Way to the next crossing road, then turn right onto this and turn right again at the next crossroads.

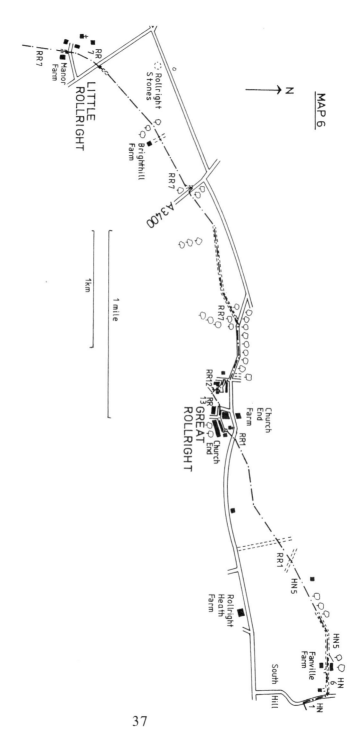

MAP 6

N

LITTLE ROLLRIGHT

Manor Farm

RR7

RR7

Rollright Stones

Brighthill Farm

RR7

A3400

RR7

RR12

RR13 GREAT ROLLRIGHT

Church End Farm

Church End

RR1

RR1

HN5

HN5

Rollright Heath Farm

Fanville Farm

HN5

HN6

HN1

South Hill

1 km

1 mile

Now take path RR7 straight on across the field to a gap in the far hedge, then keep straight on beside a sporadic left-hand hedge entering a sunken way by an ash tree and following it downhill to a gate and gap onto a road, which, despite its narrowness, was, till the construction of the modern A3400 in the 1820s, part of the Oxford - Stratford-upon-Avon turnpike road. Cross this road and go through a hedge gap opposite where the largely deserted village of Little Rollright comes into view in its hollow ahead. Here bear slightly left down the field to the near left-hand corner of the 'lost village` site then bear half left across a field corner towards a twin-poled electricity pylon to reach the road into the village.

Little Rollright - Salford (Map 7)

OS Maps
Landranger Sheets 151 & 164
Outdoor Leisure Sheet 45
Pathfinder Sheets 1044 (SP23/33) & 1068 (SP22/32)

Unlike many Oxfordshire 'lost villages`, which became depopulated due to the ravages of the Black Death or agricultural malpractice impoverishing the soil, Little Rollright was reduced to a church, a manor house and a scattering of remote farms and cottages by early inclosure in about 1500 which resulted in the forcible eviction of most of its population. Despite the fact that this deprived the tiny fifteenth-century church of most of its congregation, William Blower, a later holder of the manor, in 1617 extended the church by giving it its pinnacled tower and it has only survived thanks to the generosity of various benefactors who have ensured its upkeep.

Take path RR7 straight on across the road into Little Rollright and down a farm road into the yard of Manor Farm where you keep straight on between barns to reach a hedge gap into a field. Continue up this field to cross a stile in its top hedge, then take path SA6 following a right-hand hedge straight on with a fine view to your left towards Chipping Norton. At the far end of the field go through a hunting-gate and take an obvious path downhill through a plantation. At its far side cross a track and go through a shallow ford then follow a right-hand hedge for 120 yards to reach gates in it. Go through these and follow the other side of the hedge to a gate into another plantation. Take the obvious path through it, then cross a stile into a field and bear slightly left across it to a corner of a hedge surrounding Rectory Farm. Now follow this hedge straight on to cross a stile in a corner of the field, then bear slightly left to cross a second stile where you bear half left across a field to a stile in its far corner leading to Golden Lane on the edge of Salford.

Salford - Cornwell (Map 7)

OS Maps
Landranger Sheets 163 & 164
Outdoor Leisure Sheet 45
Pathfinder Sheet 1068 (SP22/32)

Salford, in a hollow just off the ancient London-Worcester turnpike road (now the A44), bears little resemblance to its more famous northern namesake, the home of ´Coronation Street`. The name of both is, in fact, probably a corruption of ´salt-ford` and, in the case of the Oxfordshire village, results from its proximity to the A44, part of an ancient ´salt-track` used for transporting the salt from salt-mines in the Midlands to London, essential, in the days before the invention of the freezer, to the storage of meat. The village church, which you will pass shortly, is of Norman origin but was substantially rebuilt in the fourteenth century when its tower was added.

Turn right into Golden Lane to reach a crossroads on the village green where you turn right again. At the far side of the green turn right into a cul-de-sac called The Leys. Where it bears right, take path SA3 straight on over a stile by a gate. Now bear half left going through a hedge gap under an ash tree and crossing the next field diagonally to a kissing-gate into Salford Churchyard. Here take path SA2 beside a left-hand stone wall at first, then passing left of the church to reach gates onto the church drive. Where the drive turns left, leave it and take a fenced path straight on to the A44.
   Turn right along its near verge, then, after 100 yards, just past a large road sign, turn left crossing the road and taking bridleway SA10 through a hedge gap. Now follow a grassy track bearing right then left and following a right-hand hedge to the far side of the field, then continuing past a left-hand plantation and through a second field. Where the right-hand hedge ends, follow a winding track straight on with fine views behind you towards Salford Church, soon joining a left-hand hedge. At the far side of the field ignore a branching track to your right, go through a hedge gap and ignore branching tracks to left and right, then take bridleway CO4 straight on beside a right-hand hedge, with a fine view towards Chipping Norton to your left, to reach Glebe Farm. Here follow the farm road bearing left then right to pass between the farm buildings then bearing left then right again to reach Rectory Lane.
   Turn right onto this road, then, after about 30 yards at the far

40

end of a left-hand stone wall, turn left through a gate and kissing-gate onto path CO2 following a faint grassy track downhill to cross a concrete bridge right of a tall oak tree. Now take path CO3 bearing slightly left uphill to enter a fenced track leading to a kissing-gate into Cornwell Churchyard.

Cornwell - Kingham Field (Map 7)

OS Maps
Landranger Sheet 163
Outdoor Leisure Sheet 45
Pathfinder Sheet 1068 (SP22/32)

Cornwell, in its remote Cotswold hollow, is one of several surviving examples in Oxfordshire of the estate village where virtually the whole village belongs to the owner of the manor house. This situation even resulted in 1991 in a public inquiry deciding that there was no public right of way along the main village street! The present manor house, a fine Georgian house with grounds redesigned in the 1930s by Clough Williams Ellis, replaced an earlier building which in the Civil War together with nearby Chastleton House formed a Royalist stronghold, while the tiny parish church, set in the park of the manor house, is Norman with a fifteenth-century chancel.

Take a gravel path through the churchyard passing left of the church, then continue through a kissing-gate and along a path between iron railings within an avenue of lime trees with views of the Manor House to your left. By a corner of the Manor House garden cross a stile in the right-hand fence and bear left to a corner of a fence by a walnut tree. Here ignore a gate and kissing-gate to your left and a stile to your right and rejoin path CO2 following a left-hand fence to a stile in it. Turn left over this then right through a hedge gap. Now bear half left across an orchard. At its far corner bear slightly right to join a stony track leading to a road called Narrow Lane.

Turn left and follow it downhill past the village and up again to a T-junction. Here turn left onto the Chipping Norton road, then opposite the drive to the Manor House, turn right up some steps and through a kissing-gate onto path CO7 bearing half left across a parkland field crossing a rise to reach a stile in the far left-hand corner of the field. Now bear slightly right down the next field with fine views towards Chipping Norton to your left to cross a gated culvert at a wiggle in the bottom hedge, then bear slightly left to cross a footbridge and stiles in the next hedge. Here take path KH9 bearing slightly right across the next field to pass through a gate in the next hedge and continue to gates in a tall cypress hedge leading into Kingham Hill Farm. Now take a wide farm road straight on through the farm ignoring a branching road to your right, leaving the farm through gates and bearing left with Churchill coming into view on the ridge ahead. Where the road bears right, leave it and take a grassy track beside a left-hand hedge straight on downhill. Halfway down the right-hand field, by a gap in the hedge, leave the track and bear half right across the field to cross a stile in the bottom right-hand corner onto crossing bridleway KH11.

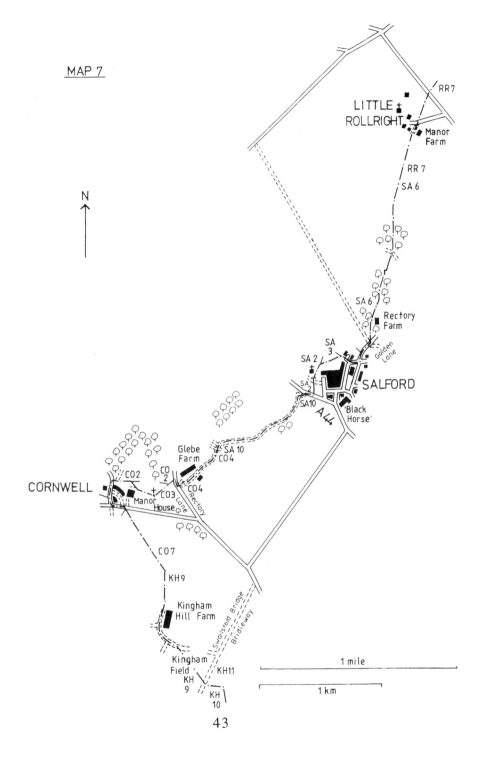

MAP 7

N

RR 7

LITTLE
ROLLRIGHT

Manor
Farm

RR 7
SA 6

SA 6

Rectory
Farm

Golden Lane

SA 3
SA 2
SALFORD
SA10
'Black
Horse'
A44

SA 10
CO4

Glebe
Farm

CO2
CO 2
CO3
CO4

CORNWELL

Manor House

Rectory Lane

CO7

KH9

Kingham
Hill Farm

Swalstord Bridge
Bridleway

Kingham
Field
KH11
KH 9
KH 10

1 mile

1 km

43

Kingham Field - Churchill (Map 8)

OS Maps
Landranger Sheet 163
Outdoor Leisure Sheet 45
Pathfinder Sheet 1068 (SP22/32)

Cross this bridleway and a stile opposite and take path KH10 following a left-hand hedge to cross a footbridge, then take path CH6 bearing half right across the next field to cross another footbridge concealed by a stunted ash tree. Now bear half right across another field to a stile leading to the former Chipping Norton Branch Line opened in 1855 and closed in 1962 and from 1887 to 1951 part of the Banbury and Cheltenham line previously encountered on the D´Arcy Dalton Way at Hook Norton.

Cross the old railway and a footbridge beyond, then bear half right across a field to a gap and footbridge in the right-hand hedge. Now bear half left over a rise to a gap in the next hedge, then bear half left across a third field to a stile into a plantation. Take the obvious path through this, descending some steps to a footbridge then climbing again to a stile where Churchill comes into view ahead and to your right is a view across the Evenlode valley towards Stow-on-the-Wold. Now bear slightly left across this field, crossing a stile in a wooden fence and continuing to a field corner where a narrow strip of field leads you to a gate and stile onto a road called Hastings Hill in Churchill.

Turn left onto this road, then, after some 70 yards, just past a left-hand stone cottage close to the road, turn right onto path CH1 up a gravel drive. Where the drive bears right, go straight on along a narrow alleyway then cross Kingham Road and continue along an enclosed grassy track right of the Methodist Church to a gate and stile into a field where a fine view opens out to your right across the Evenlode valley towards Kingham and Stow-on-the-Wold. Here turn left onto path CH4 to cross a stile in the field corner and continue to a further stile into a farmyard at Churchill Farm. Go straight on through the farmyard then continue up some steps, over a stile and along a walled path to reach Langston Close where you turn left to reach the B4450 by the ´Chequers` in the centre of Churchill.

Churchill - Sarsden (Map 8)

OS Maps
Landranger Sheets 163 & 164
Outdoor Leisure Sheet 45
Pathfinder Sheet 1068 (SP22/32)

Churchill, once a market town, has a church familiar to walkers from Oxford as its tower is a scaled-down model of Magdalen College tower, while its walls and ceiling are based on New College and Christ Church Hall respectively. Built in 1826 to replace a thirteenth-century building at the bottom of Hastings Hill of which only the chancel remains, it was designed by Squire John Haughton Langston, in whose memory the nearby ornate conduit was installed in 1863. In the eighteenth century Churchill was the birthplace of two famous men: Warren Hastings (1732 - 1818), first Governor General of India, and William Smith (1769 - 1839), a canal-builder who in 1815 published the first geological map of England and Wales and is known as the 'father of British geology'. A stone memorial to him stands on a small green in the centre of the village.

Turn right onto the B4450, then, by the church, fork left into Church Road descending out of the village to cross a bridge over Sars Brook, then continuing uphill to a road junction. Here fork right onto the road to Sarsden and follow it uphill to a T-junction by an old stone cross at Sarsden where there is a fine view back over your right shoulder towards Churchill.

Sarsden - Lyneham (Map 8)

OS Maps
Landranger Sheets 163 & 164
Outdoor Leisure Sheet 45
Pathfinder Sheet 1068 (SP22/32)

Sarsden´s mediæval Butter Cross, one of the finest ancient stone crosses in Oxfordshire, was on 27th September 1987 the scene of the opening of the D´Arcy Dalton Way by Lt. Col. Dalton´s widow, Mrs. Julia Dalton. The village, if one can call it that, consists of Sarsden House, a fine manor house of Georgian appearance but with Jacobean and older elements, and the church dating from 1760 in parkland designed by Humphrey Repton in 1795, through which you are about to pass, several scattered farms and a few cottages along the road towards Lyneham.

Here take bridleway SR3 straight on through white gates and along a fenced track, ignoring two branching tracks to your right into Home Farm, then continuing with glimpses through gaps in the right-hand hedge of Sarsden House and Church. Now disregard a crossing macadam drive and take the fenced track straight on downhill into a wood where a causeway leads you across the valley bottom and you ignore a branching bridleway to your left, then take bridleway LY8 straight on uphill out of the wood and along a green lane to Fairgreen Farm. Here take a macadam drive straight on through the farm, then at a T-junction with a farm road take a green lane straight on to a gate into a field where superb views open out to your right across the Evenlode valley towards Milton-under-Wychwood, Lyneham, Fifield, Idbury, Kingham and Stow-on-the-Wold. Now take a grassy track beside a left-hand hedge straight on to the far side of the field where you go through a fence gap where Lord Moreton´s Seat (a memorial to Henry Haughton Reynolds, Lord Moreton (1857 - 1920) who loved the magnificent panoramic view of the Evenlode valley from this point) can be reached through a gap in a stone wall to your left.

Here continue through a hedge gap looking out for the large ornamental gateposts hidden in the hedge, then go straight on across two fields, ignoring a crossing track at the end of the first and passing right of a clump of ash trees at the end of the second. Now follow a left-hand hedge straight on to pass through a hedge gap at the end of the third field then turn right onto bridleway LY7 following a farm track beside a right-hand hedge generally

MAP 8

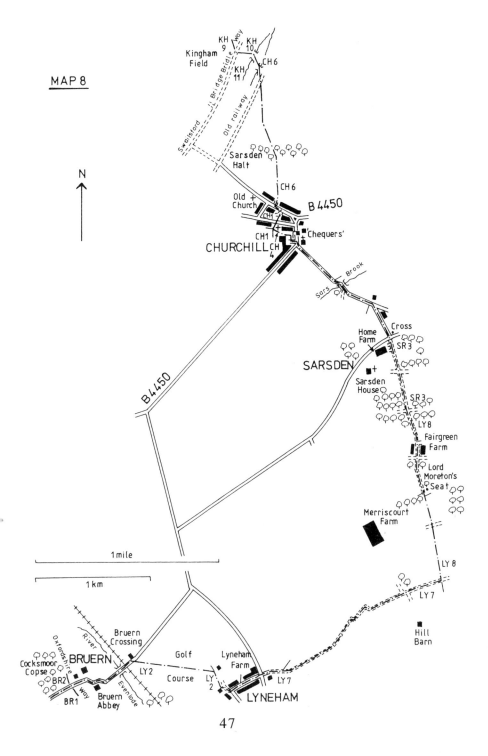

N

KH 9
KH 10
KH 11
CH 6

Kingham Field

Swailsford Bridge Bridle way

Old railway

Sarsden Halt

CH 6

Old Church

B 4450

CH 1
CH 4
'Chequers'

CHURCHILL

Sars Brook

Cross

Home Farm

SR 3

SARSDEN

Sarsden House

SR 3

B 4450

LY 8

Fairgreen Farm

Lord Moreton's Seat

Merriscourt Farm

LY 8

LY 7

1 mile

1 km

Hill Barn

Oxfordshire

River

Bruern Crossing

Golf

Course

Lyneham Farm

Cocksmoor Copse

BRUERN

BR 2

LY 2

LY 2

LY 7

BR 1

way

Bruern Abbey

Evenlode

LYNEHAM

descending gently for over a mile with more fine views across the Evenlode valley ahead and towards Merriscourt Farm to your right. In the second field you ignore a branching green lane to your right, then in the fourth you disregard a branching track and eventually you enter a green lane which becomes a macadam road and leads you to a crossroads in Lyneham.

Lyneham - Bruern (Map 8)

OS Maps
Landranger Sheet 163
Outdoor Leisure Sheet 45
Pathfinder Sheet 1068 (SP22/32)

Lyneham in the Evenlode valley, which forms the approximate halfway-mark of the D´Arcy Dalton Way, is a small attractive Cotswold village, most of which flanks the street you are about to walk. Traditionally a hamlet of Shipton-under-Wychwood, whose mediæval wealth can be seen by its magnificent church, Lyneham only became an independent parish in modern times.

Here cross the major road and go straight on down the village street. Where the street eventually turns left, turn right onto path LY2 along a gravel lane. Just past the last left-hand cottage where the track bears right, leave it and follow a left-hand stone wall to cross a footbridge onto a golf course. Here go straight on, passing left of a bunker to go through a hedge gap, then bear half left keeping just left of a green, a raised tee, a small bunker at the far side of the next fairway and another green to cross a culvert by an oak tree. Now head for a five-bar gate between the level crossing gates and the former crossing-keeper´s cottage at Bruern Crossing, passing right of a green and a pond to cross a stile by the gate onto a road.

Bruern - Fifield (Map 9)

OS Maps
Landranger Sheet 163
Outdoor Leisure Sheet 45
Pathfinder Sheets 1068 (SP22/32) & 1091 (SP21/31)

Bruern, which for walkers is quite significant as the crossing point of the D´Arcy Dalton Way and Oxfordshire Way, comprises little more than Bruern Abbey and a few cottages on a road leading to bridges over the River Evenlode. The present Bruern Abbey, built by the Cope family in the early eighteenth century on the site of a Cistercian abbey founded in 1147, was home to Sir John Cope, commander-in-chief of forces in Scotland at the time of the 1745 rebellion. Although his forces were routed by Bonny Prince Charlie at Prestonpans, Cope was not blamed for this defeat and a year later the rebellion was crushed at the Battle of Culloden. More recently, another albeit more civilised battle has been fought to save the Oxford-Worcester railway line passing the village, opened in 1853 as part of the Oxford, Worcester and Wolverhampton Railway (locally nicknamed ´The Old Worse and Worse`) and today known as the Cotswold Line.

Turn left onto the road, crossing the railway and bridges over various courses of the River Evenlode, then continue past the grounds of Bruern Abbey and a few cottages. On leaving the village, a view of Bruern Abbey opens out over your left shoulder. Now disregard the Oxfordshire Way, which crosses the road, and keep straight on, climbing gently past Cocksmoor Copse and ignoring a branching road to the right. Where woodland commences to your left, at a left-hand bend turn right through a bridlegate and take bridleway BR4 straight across a field to a hedge gap. Do **not** go through this gap, but turn left onto bridleway BR5, following a right-hand hedge to a crossing track. Turn right onto this, passing through a hedge gap, then turn left onto bridleway FI13 along a fenced track. After 150 yards, by the corner of a copse called The Firs to your left, bear half right through a fence gap and across a corner of a field heading for a large oak tree, passing through a hedge gap to rejoin the track. Now bear half left and follow it downhill beside a right-hand tree-belt. At the bottom of the field, go through a gate to reach a junction of tracks, then turn right through a hedge gap and bear half left across a field to reach a corner of Snow Hill Plantation where you join a grassy track and follow it straight on

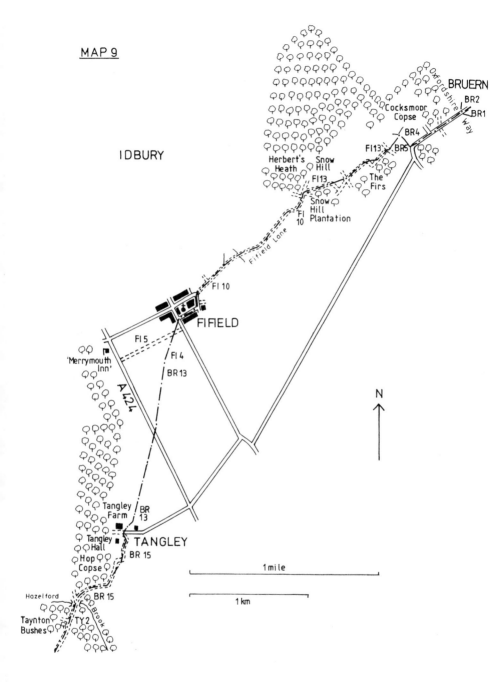

MAP 9

IDBURY

BRUERN

Cocksmoor
Copse

Herbert's
Heath

Snow
Hill

The
Firs

Snow
Hill
Plantation

Fifield Lane

FIELD

'Merrymouth
Inn'

A 424

Tangley
Farm

Tangley
Hall

Hop
Copse

Hazelford

Taynton
Bushes

TANGLEY

N

1 mile

1 km

along the edge of the wood, eventually entering the wood and reaching a five-way track junction at Snow Hill.

Here bear half left onto bridleway FI10 known as Fifield Lane, ignoring a branching track to your right then passing through a gate into a green lane. Take this lane, which can be swampy in places, straight on for three-quarters of a mile, widening into a green at one point, at the end of which you ignore a crossing path and continue, eventually passing through a gate where you keep straight on uphill to reach a small village green in Fifield.

Fifield - Tangley (Map 9)

OS Maps
Landranger Sheet 163
Outdoor Leisure Sheet 45
Pathfinder Sheet 1091 (SP21/31)

Fifield, a picturesque hillside Cotswold village near the Gloucestershire border which was once a centre for hurdle-making, was formerly known as Fifield Merrymouth after the fourteenth-century lord of the manor, John de Muremouth. The village can boast a fine Cotswold-stone manor house and thirteenth-century church with an equally ancient slender octagonal tower capped by a spire resembling a minaret. Its former name is perpetuated by the 'Merrymouth Inn' on the A424 at the top of the ridge.

At the green, fork left onto a grassy track, soon joining a macadam road. Where it forks by the gate to The Manor, bear right into Church Street uphill past the church to a T-junction. Here turn left and after 50 yards, turn right through a kissing-gate onto path FI4 leading you between a hedge and a fence to another kissing-gate into a field where fine views open out to your left towards Milton-under-Wychwood in the Evenlode valley and what remains of the ancient Royal Forest of Wychwood on the hills beyond. Now bear half right across this field, passing just right of an electricity pole to reach a hedge gap in the far corner, then bear half left across a field corner to another gap and concealed stile. Cross this and take path BR13 bearing half right across the next field, heading for a gap between a small plantation and a holly tree on the skyline to reach a gate in the far corner of the field onto the A424, which, like many Cotswold main roads, follows the crest of the ridge.

Cross this road and go through a hedge gap opposite, then take the continuation of path BR13 bearing half left across a field heading for the left-hand end of a line of trees at the far side of a second field, with views opening out ahead towards the Windrush valley and to your right towards Little Rissington airfield. At the far side of the field go through a hedge gap, then bear slightly right across the second field, heading right of a double cottage at Tangley to cross a stile, then continue across a third field to a gate by a farmhouse leading to the end of the public road at Tangley.

Tangley - Hazelford Brook (Map 9)

OS Maps
Landranger Sheet 163
Outdoor Leisure Sheet 45
Pathfinder Sheet 1091 (SP21/31)

Tangley, an outlying hamlet of Bruern parish at the end of a cul-de-sac lane on the edge of woods flanking the Gloucestershire border, is now arguably one of the remotest settlements in Oxfordshire. It would appear from earthworks in the field you have just crossed that Tangley was once much larger and, whether as a result of the Black Death or agricultural changes, the settlement at some time became depopulated. In any event, the fine Cotswold stone manor house of Tangley Hall suggests that it was once a place of some wealth.

Now cross the road and take bridleway BR15 straight on through a gate opposite, following a fenced grassy track, passing a fine row of mature walnut trees to your left and Tangley Hall in the hollow to your right, then climbing to a gate into a field. Here take a grassy track straight on beside a right-hand hedge. Where the track bears right, leave it and bear slightly right across the field to rejoin the track by a corner of Hop Copse at the top of the next rise. Now follow this grassy track straight on along the edge of the wood bearing right where it enters the next field and dropping to a field corner. Here continue steeply downhill through a neck of woodland to cross a bridge over a brook, then bear left across the corner of a field to join a farm road and cross a bridge over Hazelford Brook into a wood called Taynton Bushes.

Hazelford Brook - Great Barrington (Map 10)

OS Maps
Landranger Sheet 163
Outdoor Leisure Sheet 45
Pathfinder Sheet 1091 (SP21/31)

In Taynton Bushes take bridleway TY2 straight on up a wide farm road through this wood with its magnificent tall oak, ash and Scots pine trees. On leaving the wood, take a grassy track straight on beside a left-hand hedge for over three-quarters of a mile through four fields with fine views through gaps in the hedge in the third and fourth fields across the Hazelford valley, (where the celebrated Taynton stone used in the building of Windsor Castle, St. Paul´s Cathedral, Blenheim Palace, Burford Church, the bridges on the Oxford, Worcester and Wolverhampton Railway and many of the Oxford colleges was quarried for centuries) towards Taynton Down, Burford, Upton Down and Didcot Power Station and the Wessex Downs beyond. At the far end of the fourth field go through a hedge gap and turn right onto bridleway TY1, a track following a right-hand hedge through two fields past a ruined farm to your right. At the far end of the second field, by a fine clump of tall beech trees called Miletree Clump, bear slightly left into a green lane in Gloucestershire (bridleway BA7) with a tree-belt to your right. Halfway along the tree-belt turn left through a hedge gap with wooden gateposts onto bridleway BA8 across a field with views to your left as before but now with the part of the Downs which is your ultimate goal ahead and the distant Chilterns to the left of Didcot Power Station, heading just left of the wooden pylon right of a distant clump of trees to reach the far corner of the field.

Here bear half left through a hedge gap and take a grassy track beside a right-hand hedge through two fields. In the second field the track passes through a gap in the right-hand hedge where the Barringtons, nestling in the Windrush valley, come into view ahead. Here diverge from the left-hand hedge heading towards a wood on the skyline right of a large barn at Great Barrington to reach a large gap in the bottom hedge, then take a grassy track straight on, soon entering a sunken way and following it downhill to a gate. Go through this and continue along a causeway then take a grassy track uphill to a gate into a farmyard at Barrington Farm. By the near end of the right-hand barn, turn right onto a fenced track passing another farmyard to your left, then, just before reaching a stone shed, turn left down a macadamed lane between stone walls to reach the main village street in Great Barrington.

Great Barrington - Little Barrington (Map 10)

OS Maps
Landranger Sheet 163
Outdoor Leisure Sheet 45
Pathfinder Sheet 1091 (SP21/31)

Great Barrington, a fine Cotswold stone village of well-built mainly seventeenth- to nineteenth-century houses in the Windrush valley was, till quite recently, in a severely neglected state with some houses derelict and a tree growing through the collapsed roof of one of them. The derelict buildings have now been renovated to pristine condition so that the village once again has the well-groomed air of the wealthy estate village which it appears once to have been. To the west of the village is Barrington Park, a fine Palladian mansion built between 1736 and 1738, possibly to a design by the renowned architect William Kent, enclosed in a large landscaped garden and deer park surrounded by a high stone wall. Also within the park is the parish church of twelfth-century origin but largely rebuilt in the fifteenth century when its tower was added. The church contains a number of interesting monuments to the Bray family including one by Nollekens and the fact that it is situated within the park suggests that the original village may also have been there, but that the present houses were built to enable its demolition and the creation of the park.

Now turn right into the village street and after 70 yards, opposite house no.15, turn left down a macadamed alleyway to reach a back street. Turn right onto this passing the village school to your left, then turn left through a handgate onto path BA10 following a left-hand stone wall at first then keeping straight on to reach an electricity pole. Here bear half right with fine views ahead towards Little Barrington to reach a gate and stile in the bottom right-hand corner of the field by Barrington Mill. Now on path BA9, cross the stile and turn left along the drive to the mill passing through a gate. Where the drive ends at the mill, go straight on through a gate and across a lawn, a footbridge over one arm of the Windrush and a stile, then continue along a fenced path to cross a stile and footbridge right of a dilapidated farm bridge over another arm of the Windrush and reach the end of Minnow Lane at Little Barrington.

MAP 10

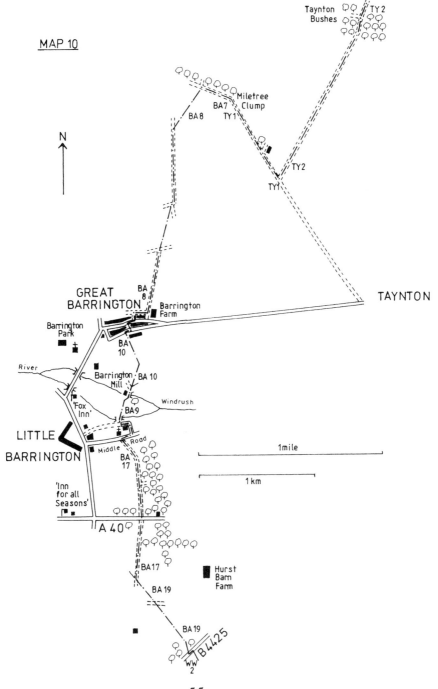

N

Taynton
Bushes
TY 2

Miletree
Clump
BA7 TY 1

BA 8

TY 2

TY 1

TAYNTON

GREAT
BARRINGTON
BA
8

Barrington
Farm

Barrington
Park

BA
10

River

Barrington
Mill   BA 10

Windrush

'Fox
Inn'
BA 9

LITTLE
BARRINGTON

Middle   Road

BA
17

1mile

1 km

'Inn
for all
Seasons'

A 40

BA17

Hurst
Barn
Farm

BA 19

BA 19

WW
2   B4425

Little Barrington - B4425 (Map 10)

OS Maps
Landranger Sheet 163
Outdoor Leisure Sheet 45
Pathfinder Sheet 1091 (SP21/31)

Little Barrington, on the opposite side of the Windrush to Great Barrington and united with it for parish purposes since 1935, is renowned for its triangular village green with a stream (once a stone quarry) surrounded by stone cottages which is one of the most picturesque scenes in the Cotswolds. Its church, to the east of the green on a narrow road towards Burford, is also of twelfth-century origin, but was largely rebuilt in the fourteenth century when its tower was added.

If wishing to visit the village green, turn right. Otherwise bear left and take the road bearing right uphill to a T-junction. Here turn right onto Middle Road, then, just before Little Barrington Church to your right, turn left through a gate onto bridleway BA17 taking a grassy track across a field to a hedge gap by the near right-hand corner of a copse called Drive Covert. Now continue uphill past the copse and across a field to a gap in the trees on the skyline where gates lead you to the A40, another ridgetop main road, once the principal road from London to Gloucester, South Wales and the ferries to the south of Ireland.

Cross this busy road carefully and take bridleway BA17 straight on through gates opposite, following a right-hand hedge through two fields passing an outcrop of woodland between the fields. In the second field, by the fourth electricity pole in the right-hand hedge, leave the track and take path BA19 bearing half left across the field to a hedge gap by a lightning-damaged hawthorn tree. Here cross a track and bear half left across the next field to its far corner where you go through one hedge gap and turn left through a second then turn right to follow a right-hand hedge past a copse called The Beeches to gates and a stile onto the B4425, Burford - Cirencester road on the Oxfordshire/Gloucestershire boundary.

B4425 - Westwell (Map 11)

OS Maps
Landranger Sheet 163
Outdoor Leisure Sheet 45
Pathfinder Sheet 1091 (SP21/31)

Cross the B4425 reentering Oxfordshire and take bridleway WW2 through a gap by gates opposite, then follow a left-hand stone wall to the far side of the field. Here bear left through a gap then follow a right-hand hedge looking out for a bridlegate in it. Turn right through this then left along the other side of the hedge to a field corner where you turn right and follow a left-hand hedge uphill to a corner of a copse called Plum Tree Covert. Here turn left through a former gateway and take a fenced track straight on past the copse to the edge of Westwell. Now cross a concrete road and a triangle of grass then take a stone track straight on to the left-hand end of a long barn. Here turn left through a former gateway and take a path between a hedge and a stone wall to enter the churchyard where you pass left of the church to reach a gap in the far corner leading to Westwell village green with its duckpond in front of you.

Westwell - Holwell (Map 11)

OS Maps
Landranger Sheet 163
Outdoor Leisure Sheet 45
Pathfinder Sheets 1091 (SP21/31) & 1115 (SP20/30)

Westwell, nestling in its quiet hollow on the down-slope of the Cotswolds, is a superb unspoilt example of the Cotswold village largely undiscovered by tourists with its sixteenth-century manor house, a late seventeenth-century former rectory, a small twelfth-century church with a wooden turret and an unusual Norman font, a churchyard with finely carved headstones and table-tombs and a collection of rose-clad stone cottages. On the green with its picturesque duckpond is also a war memorial in the form of a mediæval stone cross incorporating a brass figure `1` originating from the clock of the Cloth Hall in the Belgian town of Ypres destroyed during a bombardment in the First World War.

57

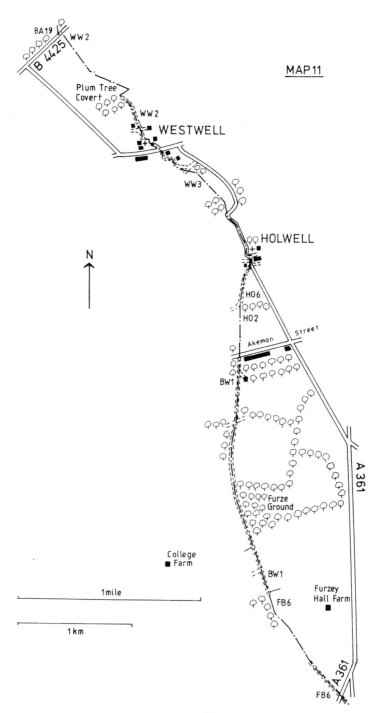

MAP 11

BA19
WW 2
B 4425

Plum Tree
Covert

WW 2

WESTWELL

WW3

HOLWELL

HO6

HO2

Akeman   Street

BW1

N

A 361

College
■ Farm

Furze
Ground

BW1

FB6

Furzey
Hall Farm

1 mile

1 km

A 361

FB6

Now turn left down a macadam drive to reach the village street by the war memorial, then cross the road and take path WW3 straight on along a macadam drive, passing an old stone cattle trough planted with flowers and bearing left then right to reach the Manor House. Here bear right again along a gravel drive crossing a stream, then bear slightly right off the drive and take a path between lime trees, ignoring a gate to your right and reaching a hunting-gate onto a cul-de-sac branch of the drive. Cross this and a stile, then bear half left through a gate and continue through three narrow fields to a gate and stile leading to a bend in a road which you follow straight on uphill to reach Holwell by the church.

Holwell - A361 Filkins Bypass (Map 11)

OS Maps
Landranger Sheet 163
Outdoor Leisure Sheet 45
Pathfinder Sheet 1115 (SP20/30)

Holwell, an attractive tiny Cotswold village with more rose-clad stone cottages and a nineteenth-century church and former village school, lies just off Akeman Street, an ancient Roman road from London via Watford, Aylesbury and Bicester to Cirencester. Historically, the village was a hamlet of Broadwell, 3.5 miles to the south and the next section of the Way largely retraces the villagers´ steps along what is known as Deadman´s Walk to reach its imposing parish church. It is presumed that this name originated because it was necessary to carry coffins this way for burial at the parish church.

At the fork by Holwell War Memorial go right, then ignore a branching track to your right and continue past the former village school. Now bear half right onto a fenced track (HO6) and follow it for a quarter mile. By the end of a stone wall and tree-belt to your left, fork left through a gate and the tree-belt onto bridleway HO2, then continue beside a right-hand hedge to a bridlegate onto Akeman Street with a fine avenue of lime trees to your right.

Cross this road and take bridleway BW1 straight on along a stone track, initially walled on both sides but later only to the right. Where the track forks, follow the stone wall straight on, then, where the wall ends, continue along a green lane for a quarter mile, eventually emerging into a left-hand field. Here take the grassy track straight on beside a right-hand line of trees and a stone wall, entering another green lane where a wood called Furze Ground commences to your left. Where the right-hand hedge turns away to your right, a fine view opens out ahead across the Thames Valley towards Coleshill and the Downs and you continue along the grassy track through two fields beside the wood then a left-hand hedge, ignoring a branching bridleway to your right in the second field. At the far end of this field disregard a branching track to your right and take the grassy track straight on across a third field to a hedge gap. Here ignore a branching bridleway to your left and take bridleway FB6 straight on through a hedge gap and beside a right-hand hedge. Having passed a mid-field oak to your left, by a waymarking post bear half left across the field to a gap in the far hedge where the spire of Broadwell Church comes into view ahead. Now go straight on across the next field, heading midway between the church spire and an oak tree in a hedge ahead to pass through a hedge gap, then follow a grassy track beside a right-hand hedge at first towards Broadwell Church and continuing to a gate onto the A361 Filkins Bypass.

A361 Filkins Bypass - Filkins (Map 12)

OS Maps
Landranger Sheet 163
Outdoor Leisure Sheet 45
Pathfinder Sheet 1115 (SP20/30)

Cross this fast road carefully and take the continuation of bridleway FB6 straight on through gates opposite and along a grassy track beside a right-hand hedge to a gate onto the old main road into Filkins. Turn right onto this road and follow it for 250 yards. At a left-hand bend, turn right through a gate onto path FB8, following a left-hand hedge downhill, then at a corner bearing left to join a right-hand fence enclosing a stream. On reaching a gated culvert over the stream, turn right over it then bear left across a meadow to a gate right of a willow copse. Here go straight on through a scrubby field to cross a stile in a stone wall, then turn left onto a grassy track crossing a stone bridge. Now bear slightly right to cross a stone-stile by a cypress tree and continue between stone walls to the main village street in Filkins.

Filkins - Broadwell (Map 12)

OS Maps
Landranger Sheet 163
Outdoor Leisure Sheet 45
Pathfinder Sheet 1115 (SP20/30)

Filkins, a village of fascinating Cotswold-stone cottages built along a network of lanes flanking the ancient Burford - Lechlade turnpike road, despite its Cotswold appearance, is situated in the broad Upper Thames Valley into which you have gradually descended. Although the village has always been in close proximity to its tiny neighbour Broughton Poggs, an ancient parish with a Norman church, with their boundary having long been barely perceptible, Filkins was traditionally another hamlet of the once sizeable parish of Broadwell and since 1857 has had its own church, built in his favoured French Gothic style by the celebrated Wantage-born architect George Street (who went on to design the Law Courts in London). More recently the village was the home of Sir Stafford Cripps, Chancellor of the Exchequer in the post-war Labour government, who left his mark on the

village by building some good-quality stone council houses in 1928 to demonstrate that council houses could be designed to blend in with a traditional village and establishing a museum of rural life, while his son continued in his father´s philanthropic footsteps by converting old barns for use as craft workshops.

Turn right into the village street, then, just past The Post House, turn left into Hazells Lane and follow this quiet narrow lane lined with stone cottages to a T-junction with the B4477. Cross this road and take path FB3 straight on through a hedge gap following a left-hand hedge to the far end of the field. Here turn left over a stile by a gate onto path FB1, following a left-hand hedge to another gate. Go through this and take path BW4 bearing slightly right across the next field to cross a stile about 30 yards to the right of a gate into Kings Lane. Now cross a stone stile opposite and take path BW2 following a left-hand fence towards Broadwell Church. Where the fence bears left, leave it and go straight on to cross a stile by a hawthorn bush, then continue past a fine maple tree to reach a track. Turn right onto this, soon with a fine view of the Georgian manor house to your left, then, by a stone building, turn left off the track and follow a line of poplar trees to a gate into the church-yard. Now take a gravel path through the churchyard, passing right of the church to reach gates onto Broadwell´s village street.

Broadwell - Little Clanfield (Map 12)

OS Maps
Landranger Sheet 163
Outdoor Leisure Sheet 45
Pathfinder Sheet 1115 (SP20/30)

Broadwell (locally pronounced ´Braddle´) with its superb twelfth-century church with a massive thirteenth-century spire gives the impression of being a place of mediæval wealth and the table-tombs in the churchyard with their rolled ´wool bale´ tops may indicate that, like many of the Cotswold towns with their fine stone houses and churches, Broadwell´s wealth derived from sheep-farming for the Flanders weavers. Less than 100 yards to your left when you leave the churchyard is the boundary with the neighbouring village of Kencot, a frequent winner in best-kept village competitions, which also has a Norman church but of less pretentious proportions to that of Broadwell.

Cross the village street and take path BW7 straight on along a gravel drive passing through two gates to reach a field where you bear slightly right past an attractive pond to a further gate. Now bear slightly right across a narrowing field to a gate at its far end, then follow a right-hand hedge looking out for a footbridge in it. Here do **not** cross this bridge, but bear slightly left across the field to a stile and footbridge over Langhat Ditch under a willow tree in the middle of the far hedge. Cross these and a further stile, then take path AV19 bearing half right across the next field to the right-hand corner of a copse where you bear right joining path AV14 to cross a stile by a gate just right of Lower Rookshill Farm. Now take a farm road straight on beside a left-hand hedge for a third of a mile to reach a T-junction of farm roads by a bridge carrying Calcroft Lane over the former East Gloucestershire Railway from Oxford to Fairford, built in 1873 and closed by Dr. Beeching in 1962 and locally known as the 'Fairford Flyer'. Here turn right and follow a farm road to a gate and stile onto Calcroft Lane.

Turn right onto this road and after 40 yards turn left over a stile onto path BW12 bearing slightly left across a field to a stile onto the old railway (now a farm road). Cross these and take path BW12a straight on across a large field to reach the corner of a hedge by a hedge gap. Do **not** go through this gap, but follow the left-hand hedge straight on for a quarter mile with views towards Coleshill to your right, looking out for a footbridge and stiles in the hedge. Turn left over these then right and take path CF10 following the hedge and stream at first. Where these bear right, leave them and bear slightly right across the field to pass through a gate by an ash tree, then turn left and follow a left-hand hedge to go through another gate. Now bear slightly right across the next field heading towards a farm at Little Clanfield to pass through a gate in the next hedge, then keep straight on, heading between the farm and a stone cottage, crossing a stile and reaching a road at Little Clanfield.

Little Clanfield - Langley Lane (Map 12)

OS Maps
Landranger Sheet 163
Outdoor Leisure Sheet 45
Pathfinder Sheet 1115 (SP20/30)

Little Clanfield, at the end of a mile-long cul-de-sac lane, is today, like its near neighbour Grafton, a collection of scattered farms and cottages, but pre-inclosure maps suggest that both hamlets were once larger and that inclosure in the 1830s and 1840s may have caused or contributed to their depopulation.

Cross this road and take path CF9 straight on through a hedge gap and beside a right-hand willow copse. At the far end of the copse, turn right and follow the winding field edge until, near the far side of the field, you reach a footbridge to your right. Turn right over this and take path CF14 bearing slightly left across a large field, passing just right of the first wooden electricity pylon then left of a line of four to reach a hedge gap leading to a green lane. Continue along this, passing a cottage to your right, then soon joining a farm road which you follow straight on to reach Langley Lane.

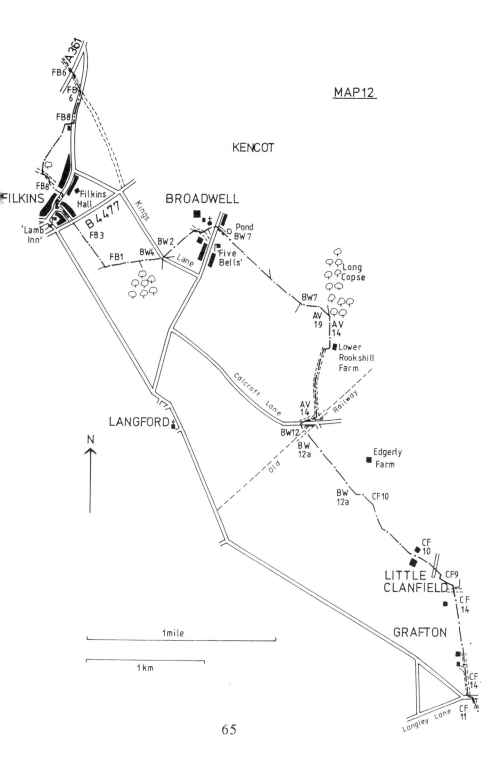

MAP 12

FB6
FB 6
FB8

KENCOT

FILKINS
FB8
Filkins
Hall
B4477
'Lamb
Inn'
FB 3
FB1
BW4
BW2

Kings
Lane

BROADWELL
Pond
BW7
'Five
Bells'

Long
Copse

BW7
AV
19
AV
14

Lower
Rookshill
Farm

N

Calcroft Lane

AV
14
Railway
LANGFORD
BW12

BW
12a
Edgerly
Farm

Old

BW
12a
CF10

CF
10

LITTLE
CLANFIELD
CF9

CF
14

GRAFTON

1 mile

1 km

CF
14

Langley Lane
CF
11

65

Langley Lane - Radcot (Map 13)

OS Maps
Landranger Sheet 163
Outdoor Leisure Sheet 45 & Explorer Sheet 170
Pathfinder Sheets 1115 (SP20/30) & 1135 (SU29/39)

Turn left into Langley Lane, then, after 30 yards, turn right onto path CF11, following a concrete road for a third of a mile, which bears left (becoming path GR1) and continues to Radcot Bridge Farm. Here bear half left onto a gravel track passing left of the farm and joining a right-hand hedge. At a field corner go straight on through a hedge gap and over a culvert, then leave the track and bear half left across a large field with views of Folly Hill, Faringdon to your right, passing just left of a wooden pylon, ignoring a crossing bridleway in mid-field and continuing until you reach a farm road just right of the far corner of the field. Turn left onto this then right through a gate and over a culvert. Here turn left over a stile and bear half right, disregarding a gated culvert to your left but noticing the earthworks to which it leads, known as 'The Garrison' believed to be a camp created by Prince Rupert in 1645 in his defence of Radcot Bridge against Parliamentary forces. Now continue to a footbridge on the Thames Path on the edge of Radcot.

Radcot - Eaton Hastings (Map 13)

OS Maps
Landranger Sheet 163
Explorer Sheet 170
Pathfinder Sheet 1135 (SU29/39)

Radcot, on the A4095 Witney - Faringdon road, has been the site of a bridge across the Thames for over 1000 years, as a Saxon chronicle refers to one already in existence in 958A.D. Since 1787, however, when attempts were made to improve the navigability of the Upper Thames by digging a new channel, there have been two bridges at Radcot, the more northerly one dating from that year, while the more southerly one, believed to be the oldest surviving bridge on the Thames, is thought to date from the thirteenth century. As one of the few bridges over the Thames in mediæval times, Radcot Bridge was of strategic importance and in 1387 the rebellious Henry Bolingbroke demolished its central

arch in order to cut off Richard II's forces under the Earl of Oxford, who were subsequently routed, while during the Civil War it was the scene of a series of skirmishes between 1644 and 1646 before ultimately succumbing to Parliamentary control. Both bridges, which are said to be haunted by the ghost of a boatman beheaded by a local farmer whose sheep he stole, are built of Taynton stone and the gardens of the 'Swan Inn' mark the site of a wharf where this stone was loaded for use further downstream, while nearby is a seventeenth-century manor house.

At the riverbank turn left over the footbridge on the Thames Path (GR6) to reach a gate onto the A4095 by the newer of the two bridges. Here turn right onto this road crossing both hump-backed bridges and leaving the Thames Path behind. Now in what till 1974 was Berkshire but has since been Oxfordshire, at the far end of the older second bridge, turn right over a stile by a disused gate onto path GF6 following a slight causeway near the bank of the Thames at first with views ahead towards Badbury Hill and Coleshill, then bearing slightly left to pass left of an electricity pylon and cross a stile in the far left-hand corner of the field. Now follow a right-hand hedge straight on with views of Folly Hill to your left, looking out for a stile to your right into a spinney. Cross this and go through the spinney passing right of a pond, then cross a stile near a windpump and take path GF7 beside a right-hand fence through three fields past Camden Farm to your left, bearing slightly left at the far end of the third field to cross a stile and footbridge.

Now take fenced path EH3 to a footbridge and stile into a field where you follow the right-hand hedge straight on at first. By a gate in this hedge bear slightly left towards Lower House Farm, passing the site of Church Hill Farm to your right, to cross a foot-bridge and stiles. Now bear slightly right across a field, heading right of the farm to cross a footbridge and rail-stiles under a willow tree, then bear slightly left across a field to the left-hand corner of a silage clamp at the farm enclosed by a wall of sleepers. Here cross a rail-stile and go straight on between the silage clamp and a slurry lagoon, ignoring gates to your right, passing through a gateway and crossing a rail-stile by a New Zealand (barbed-wire) gate onto a farm road. Now bear half right to a gateway to the farmhouse, then left to cross a stile into a field where you follow a powerline straight on to a twin-poled pylon. Here join a right-hand hedge by Eaton Hastings House and follow it to cross a stile leading to the end of a public road by Eaton Hastings Church to your right.

67

Eaton Hastings - Buscot Park (Map 13)

OS Maps
Landranger Sheet 163
Explorer Sheet 170
Pathfinder Sheet 1135 (SU29/39)

Eaton Hastings with its compact Norman church, its manor house and scattered farms and cottages near the river and a small Victorian settlement on the A417 about a mile to the southwest is thought to be another deserted village site, but little appears to be known about the date of and reasons for its depopulation.

Take this road straight on, bearing left by the gate to Ferry Cottage and right at a T-junction. At a further junction by a postbox go straight on, then, at a right-hand bend, fork left onto path EH5 following a green lane to a gate, then continuing along a grassy track. Where the track bears right, leave it and follow a right-hand electric fence, soon crossing a tubed section of it and following a tree-lined left-hand stream to cross a footbridge and rail-stiles at the far end of the field. Now follow a right-hand hedge, later a fence straight on to cross a rail-stile by gates, then bear slightly right across the next field heading towards gates by the right-hand corner of Stud Farm. Having passed a fenced enclosure to your right, bear right to cross a stile right of the gates onto a concrete road. Here cross another stile opposite, then turn left and follow the left-hand hedge to a fenced farm compound, around which you turn right then left to reach a further stile. Now bear half right across the next field, passing just right of the first wooden pylon and the former Eaton Hastings School with its bell-turret to cross a stile and footbridge and reach the A417 Faringdon - Lechlade road opposite an imposing stone house dated 1893 with the village war memorial in front of it. Cross the road and turn right onto its footway, then, after 200 yards turn left between ornamental gateposts by a lodge into Buscot Park and take bridleway EH7 along a private road crossing a bridge over the end of The Lake.

MAP 13

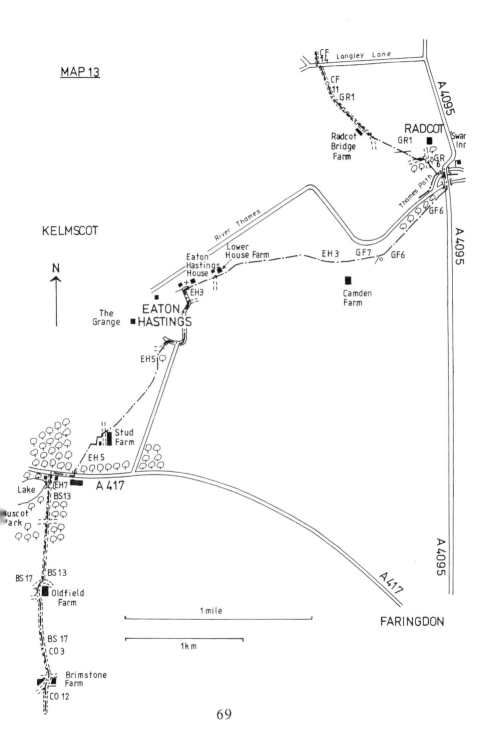

Buscot Park - Brimstone Farm (Map 13)

OS Maps
Landranger Sheet 163
Explorer Sheet 170
Pathfinder Sheet 1135 (SU29/39)

Buscot Park House, which is hidden by trees at the far end of the lake, is a beautifully-restored stately home in the Adam style built in about 1770 when the landscaped park and lake were also created. Now owned by the National Trust and open to the public in spring and summer, the house boasts fine collections of furniture and paintings including works by the Pre-Raphaelite artist Sir Edward Burne-Jones who made frequent visits to his friend and partner William Morris at his country retreat in Kelmscot just across the river.

Continue along the private road (now on bridleway BS13) for a further half mile, passing a small Doric temple and a picturesque cricket ground to your right, to reach Oldfield Farm. Where the road forks in front of the farm, bear right onto path BS17 and follow what becomes a concrete road passing right of the farm buildings and ignoring a branching track and a farm road to Heath Barn Farm. Now bear left then right and continue for nearly half a mile (soon on path CO3), with views of Badbury Hill to your left and Coleshill to your right, to reach Brimstone Farm.

Brimstone Farm - Coleshill (Map 14)

OS Maps
Landranger Sheet 163
Explorer Sheet 170
Pathfinder Sheet 1135 (SU29/39)

At the farm go straight on, ignoring all branching farm roads, then continue along a concrete road (now path CO12). After a third of a mile the road bends sharply right and then left. On rounding the left-hand bend, turn immediately right through a hedge gap onto path CO13 and take a grassy track beside a right-hand hedge. Where the track bears right into Fern Copse, leave it and follow the edge of the wood to a field corner. Here cross a footbridge by an oak tree, then continue along the edge of the wood. By a corner of the wood, ignore a hedge gap to your right and follow a right-hand hedge uphill to the edge of Cuckoopen Plantation. Here turn right through a hedge gap with superb views opening out ahead and to your right across Buscot Park and the Thames Valley towards the Cotswolds. Now follow the outside edge of the wood through two fields, gradually bearing left. Where the wood edge bears right, turn left onto a fenced path through the wood to a gate and stile onto the B4019, where Coleshill village is a quarter mile to your right.

Coleshill - Longcot (Map 14)

OS Maps
Landranger Sheet 163 or 174
Explorer Sheet 170
Pathfinder Sheet 1135 (SU29/39)

Coleshill, a hillside village named after the nearby River Cole which forms the Wiltshire boundary, today boasts an attractive small green with the remains of an ancient cross and a much-restored Norman church with a fifteenth-century tower. Until 1952, however, Coleshill was an estate village ranged around a manor house built for Sir George Pratt between 1650 and 1662 to a design by the renowned architect Inigo Jones and said to be one of the latter´s finest works, but, in that year the house, which had later passed to the Pleydell-Bouverie family, one of whom was made Earl of Radnor in 1765, was destroyed by fire and its ruins were demolished so that all that now remains are the park,

71

gateposts, stables and a dovecot. Monuments to the Pleydell-Bouverie family can be found in the parish church, while the ʾRadnor Armsˋ recalls their title and coat of arms.

Now cross the B4019 and turn left onto its far verge, following the wall of Coleshill Park for over a quarter mile, passing ornamental gates into the park. Soon after the woodland to your left ends and a superb view opens out towards Badbury Hill ahead and across Buscot Park and the Thames Valley towards the Cotswolds to your left, fork right onto bridleway CO10, the drive to Ashen Copse Farm still beside the Coleshill Park wall with fine views soon opening out ahead towards the Downs and later Great Coxwell with its prominent church to your left. Having passed two fine cedars within the park walls and gates into the park, you finally leave the park behind and drop down to Ashen Copse Farm. Here ignore a crossing path and take a farm road straight on past the farm, soon losing its macadam surface, passing Ashen Copse Wood to your right and Ashen Copse Cottages to your left and continuing along a newly-planted avenue of trees to a hedge gap and culvert. Now on bridleway LT8, take a track gently uphill through avenues of newly-planted trees across two fields, then more steeply along a lane with sporadic hedges to reach Tithe Farm. Here keep right at a fork passing right of the buildings with a fine view of White Horse Hill opening out ahead, then bear left and continue along the farm road, now with fine views of Badbury Hill and Great Coxwell to your left and the Downs to your right in places, to reach the A420.

Cross this road carefully and take the continuation of bridleway LT8 straight on through a gap opposite, then between a right-hand fence and a line of posts with fine views towards the Downs ahead and Longcot with its prominent church tower to your left. Eventually the bridleway becomes enclosed first by a left-hand, then a right-hand hedge and you continue along a green lane for over a quarter mile, looking out for the footbridge of a crossing path to your left. Turn left over this bridge and a rail-stile onto path LT6, bearing slightly right across a field to a rail-stile and footbridge over the River Ock between clumps of willow trees, then bear half left across the next field, heading some way right of a thatched stone cottage at Longcot to cross a footbridge just left of the far corner of the field. Here turn left over a second footbridge and stile onto path LT5 beside a right-hand hedge to cross a stile by a gate. Now continue across a small recreation ground and along a gravel track to reach King's Lane in Longcot, onto which you turn right.

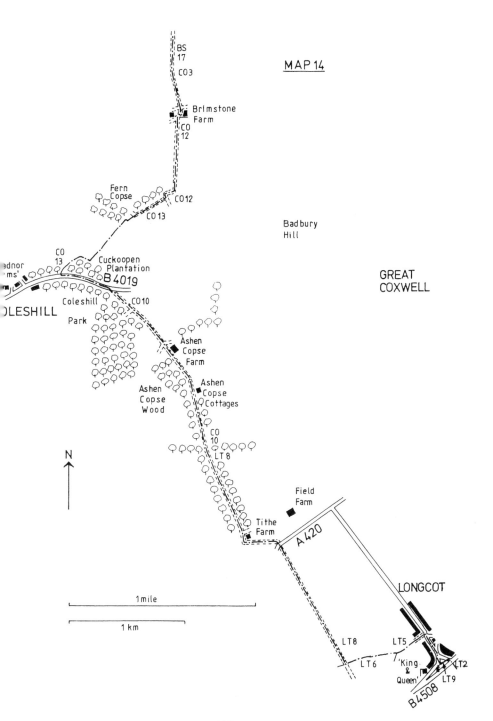

MAP 14

73

Longcot - Compton Beauchamp (Map 15)

OS Maps
Landranger Sheet 174
Explorer Sheet 170
Pathfinder Sheets 1135 (SU29/39) & 1154 (SU28/38)

Longcot, in the wide flat upper reaches of the Ock valley, better
known today as the Vale of the White Horse (since 1974 also the
name of the local District Council), offers fine views of Uffington´s
White Horse, which is of unknown origin but believed to date
either from the Iron Age or the Saxon period. The thirteenth-
century church with a kingpost roof and Jacobean pulpit, whose
eighteenth-century tower is a landmark for miles around in this
flat country, houses a memorial to Ernest Carter and his wife,
Lilian, who drowned when the ´Titanic` sank in 1912. Although
they did not live in Longcot, but in Whitechapel, East London,
where Ernest was the vicar of St. Jude´s Church, their memorial
was moved here from Whitechapel by Lilian´s uncle, John
Hughes, the vicar of Longcot, when St. Jude´s was demolished.
Lilian, whose father was the writer Tom Hughes, well-known as
the author of ´Tom Brown´s Schooldays`, is also said to have been
offered the last place in the last lifeboat to leave the ´Titanic` but to
have declined it in favour of someone else in order not to be
separated from her husband.

Where King´s Lane forks near the church, take Shrivenham Road
bearing slightly right, then turn left through the church gates onto
path LT9 to the church door. Now bear left to a gate leading to a
road junction. Here turn right, crossing the B4508 and taking path
LT2 over a stile by a gate opposite, then follow a grassy track
parallel to the right-hand hedge straight on across two fields (soon
on path LT3). In the third field continue along the track bearing
slightly left to pass the corner of a protruding hedge, then go
through a gate where you ignore a track merging from the left and
continue to a hedge gap into a fifth field. Here leave the track and
bear slightly left, passing left of a cattle trough to a gap in the far
hedge where you cross a stile and footbridge over the River Ock.
  Now take path WS7, bearing slightly left across a large field to a
railway arch bearing the old GWR main line from London to
Bristol and beyond. Go under this arch noticing how the original
arch of 1840 was extended when the line was widened from two to
four tracks in the 1880s, then keep straight on across the next field

to a footbridge and stiles where there is a fine view towards White
Horse Hill ahead. Here go straight on across a field, where you can
now barely perceive the line of the former Wilts and Berks Canal,
which opened in 1810 to link the Thames at Abingdon to the Avon
near Bath, but closed in 1914 as it could not compete with the
parallel railway and has now partially been filled in, reaching the
end of a hedge by a single oak tree. Now follow the right-hand side
of this hedge to a gateway into Claypit Lane. Cross this road and a
footbridge and stile opposite, then bear slightly left across a large
field to reach a hedge gap leading to Marsh Way, the road to
Woolstone, left of a pond in the far corner of the field.

Here do **not** join the road, but turn right onto path WS10, crossing the corner of the field to join a left-hand hedge and following
it to a field corner. Now go straight on over a stile and footbridge
and bear slightly left across the next field with a fine close-up view
of White Horse Hill to your left, to reach the far left-hand corner of
the field, where you cross three stiles and an old road called
Hardwell Lane and take path CB7, bearing half left across a field to
a stile in the far left-hand corner by the right-hand corner of the
moat at Hardwell Farm. Here bear slightly left across the next field
to its far left-hand corner where you cross a stile, a farm road and a
second stile virtually opposite then head for a thatched cottage to
cross a further stile. Now bear half left to a currently redundant
stile onto Knighton Road on the edge of Knighton. Turn right onto
this road, then immediately left through a gate onto bridleway CB2
and follow a left-hand tree-belt through two fields. Where the tree-
belt ends, take a grassy track straight on to a gate leading to a bend
in Shrivenham Road at Compton Beauchamp.

Compton Beauchamp - Wayland's Smithy (Map 15)

OS Maps
Landranger Sheet 174
Explorer Sheet 170
Pathfinder Sheet 1154 (SU28/38)

Compton Beauchamp, in its sheltered leafy hollow at the foot of the Downs, today comprises little more than a church, a manor house and a row of cottages, the majority of its parishioners living in the nearby hamlet of Knighton. The imposing Compton House is of Georgian appearance but is understood to be older while the nearby church of St. Swithun dates from the thirteenth century and has a squat fifteenth-century tower, its main treasure being some fine fourteenth-century glass. Its relatively rare dedication to the Saxon, St. Swithun, famous for his saint's day whose weather is said to be indicative of the rest of the summer, however, suggests that the present church replaced an earlier building.

Take Shrivenham Road straight on, passing the drive to Compton House to your left, then, at a right-hand bend, take the road to the church straight on. At a fork keep right, passing a barn with a clock tower and continuing along macadam path CB1 to gates to the tiny whitewashed church. Here turn right through a hunting gate and follow the churchyard fence at first, then bear slightly left across the field to a gate. Now bear half right across the next field, passing a corner of Home Copse to your right and keeping straight on, crossing a wooden fence and continuing to a hedge gap in the far corner of the field. Go through this and take path AS7 straight on beside a left-hand hedge through two fields with fine views across the Vale towards Swindon ahead and Shrivenham, Watchfield and Coleshill to your right. In the second field follow the hedge, bearing left at one point, then, where it ends, bear slightly right across the field to cross a footbridge and stiles in the valley bottom. Now take a fenced track straight on uphill beside a left-hand hedge to the top corner of the right-hand field where you join bridleway AS20 and follow it along a short green lane to a gate and stile. Here turn left through a second gate and soon bear slightly left to reach a farm road which you follow gently uphill past Odstone Farm, ignoring a crossing farm road and continuing with views to your right into Wiltshire towards Charlbury Hill and Swindon to

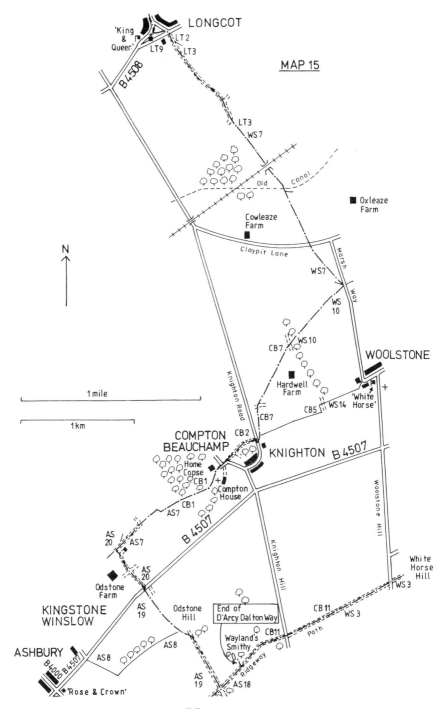

reach the B4507 on the line of the ancient Icknield Way.

Cross this road bearing slightly right and take AS19, a sunken way through scrub up Odstone Hill. On emerging from the scrub, it is worth climbing the right-hand bank to the stile of a branching path for fine views across three counties (Oxfordshire, Wiltshire and Gloucestershire). Now continue along the sunken way which soon merges with a farm road where the ground levels out. Follow this straight on for a third of a mile with fine views over your right shoulder similar to those from the stile and to your left towards Wayland's Smithy in its clump of trees. On reaching the Ridgeway (byway AS18), turn left into this green lane, thought to be at least 5000 years old and thus one of the most ancient highways in the world, and follow it for nearly 300 yards, then turn left through gates and take a fenced permissive path to your journey's end at Wayland's Smithy.

Wayland's Smithy, which may be even older than the Ridgeway itself, is an extremely well-preserved Neolithic chambered long barrow believed to date from about 3400 B.C. built over an earlier barrow thought to be some 300 years older and now surrounded by a ring of trees. Its name is, however, of Saxon origin deriving from a mythical smith called Weland. Legend has it that if a horse which has lost a shoe is left tethered at the Smithy for ten minutes, a silver coin is left and the rider whistles three times, Weland will shoe the horse and take the silver in payment. First opened in 1919, the Smithy was further excavated and restored to its present condition in 1962-3.

Access to Wayland's Smithy

The nearest regular public transport to or from Wayland's Smithy is the bus service from Swindon to Ashbury which currently operates from Monday to Saturday and on Summer Sundays, but it is advisable to contact Oxfordshire County Council's Public Transport Section on 01865-810405 before setting out to check details. A footpath route between Ashbury and Wayland's Smithy via paths AS8, AS19 and AS18 is shown on Map 15.

Circular Walk No. 1   Claydon

Length of Walk: 5.6 miles / 9.1 Km
Starting Point: T-junction by Claydon Church.
Grid Ref: SP457500
Maps: OS Landranger Sheet 151
OS Explorer Sheet 206
OS Pathfinder Sheets 999 (SP45/55) & 1022
(SP44/54)
How to get there / Parking: Claydon, 6 miles north of
Banbury, may be reached from the town by taking the
A423 towards Southam for over 4 miles, then turning
right onto a road signposted to Claydon. In the village, at
the T-junction by the church turn left towards Boddington
and Fenny Compton and find a suitable place to park.

Claydon, on its low hilltop with Northamptonshire to the east and
Warwickshire to the west, is the most northerly village in Oxfordshire and being at the watershed between tributaries of the Severn
and the Thames at the summit of the Oxford Canal, this is not just
an arbitrary historical boundary but a geographically logical
one which can be said to divide the South from the Midlands.
Nevertheless, Claydon with its attractive ironstone cottages is
typical of villages in the Oxfordshire Redlands and can boast a
Norman church with a squat fourteenth-century tower and the
Bygones Museum at Butlin Farm which displays items from rural
life in the nineteenth and early twentieth centuries. Despite its
rural setting, however, Claydon also illustrates the effects on the
countryside of the industrial revolution as, to the east and north is
the Oxford Canal, first planned in 1768 to link the River Thames
to waterways in the Midlands and provide a more reliable way to
deliver goods, in particular coal, to Banbury, Oxford and the
upper Thames Valley, which opened north of Banbury in 1778
and reached Oxford and the Thames in 1790. Designed by the
renowned canal builder James Brindley, the Oxford Canal was
initially a great success, more than halving the price of coal in
Banbury overnight, but the completion of the Grand Junction
Canal, which provided a more direct route from the Midlands to
London, and the building of the railways reduced its economic
importance and today it only carries pleasure boats. Also, to the

CIRCULAR WALK NO. 1

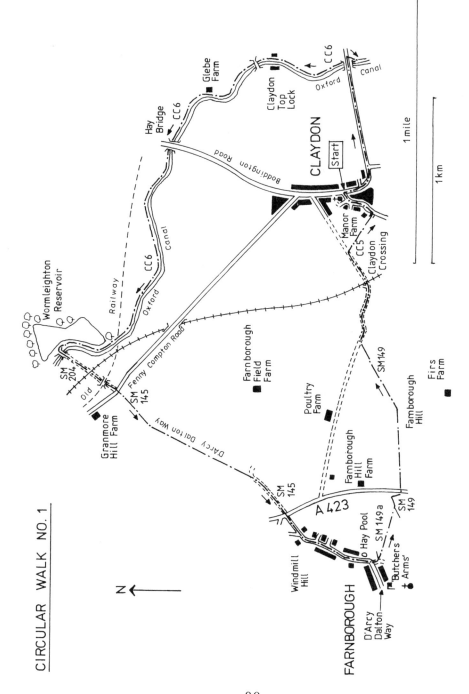

80

north near Fenny Compton is one of the many rural railway junctions which mushroomed in the mid to late nineteenth century giving strategic significance to previously remote locations, then gradually descended into a kind of enchanted slumber until the notorious Dr. Beeching finally sealed their fate.

This walk first takes you eastwards out of Claydon descending gently with fine views to the Oxford Canal, then following its towpath northwestwards for two miles into Warwickshire to reach Wormleighton Reservoir, haven for waterfowl and starting point of the D´Arcy Dalton Way, and the point of convergence of the old railways south of Fenny Compton. You then take the first mile and a half of the D´Arcy Dalton Way southwestwards to the Warwickshire village of Farnborough before returning eastwards into Oxfordshire with more fine views to reach Claydon.

Starting from the T-junction by Claydon Church take the Cropredy and Chipping Warden road past the Bygones Museum and out of the village, then, at a fork, go left towards Appletree and Chipping Warden with fine views ahead across the valley into Northamptonshire. After nearly half a mile cross a hump-backed bridge over the Oxford Canal, then turn sharp right through a small car park and a squeeze-stile by a gate onto its towpath (CC6). Turn right onto this, going under the bridge and following the towpath for two miles, passing the last three of a series of five locks which raise the level of the canal by over 30 feet to its summit, then going under bridge no.144 and continuing with views to your left towards Claydon on its hilltop in places. On nearing bridge no.143 (Hay Bridge), a view briefly opens out to your right towards the Boddingtons. You then continue onto a particularly rural section of the canal passing under the road bridge, over a brick bridge over a canal feeder from Boddington Reservoir and, on rounding a sharp right-hand bend and approaching farm drawbridge no.141, crossing into Warwickshire. Having passed between bridge piers of a former railway bridge bearing the East & West Junction Railway from Bedford to Stratford-upon-Avon, built in the 1860s and closed by Dr. Beeching 100 years later, the embankment of Wormleighton Reservoir commences to your right. Just before bridge no.139, turn right through a small gate to reach the bank of the reservoir, one of three in three different counties feeding water to the summit of the nearby Oxford Canal, and starting point of the D´Arcy Dalton Way.

Having admired the peaceful setting of the reservoir, take the D´Arcy Dalton Way (bridleway SM204) over the canal bridge and through gates, then follow a left-hand hedge to a gated level-

81

crossing over the Oxford & Birmingham Railway built in 1852. Cross this by way of its white-painted bridlegates, then continue beside the left-hand hedge through another gate and an archway bearing the former East & West Junction Railway to reach a bridlegate onto Fenny Compton Road. Here take bridleway SM145 through a gate opposite bearing slightly right across a first field to a gate. Now go straight on across a second field towards two gates right of a hedge corner. Do **not** go through these but instead bear left through a second pair of gates into a third field and bear half right across the field to gates in its far corner where Farnborough comes into view ahead and there are views towards Wormleighton behind you. Now go straight on across the next field towards Farnborough to a gate where you follow a right-hand fence straight on to join a farm road at a bend. Here take this farm road with views to your left towards Claydon, climbing gently to reach the A423, Banbury to Coventry road, on the edge of Farnborough.

Farnborough (Warks.), not to be confused with its Hampshire namesake of airshow fame, is a quiet village in a ridgetop hollow off the A423 with picturesque ironstone cottages, some thatched. The village is best-known for Farnborough Hall, an eighteenth-century classical house owned by the National Trust and can also boast a twelfth-century church largely rebuilt in the fourteenth century with its distinctive spire silhouetted against the sky.

Cross the A423 and take the Farnborough and Avon Dassett road straight on uphill into Farnborough with fine views across three counties behind you. In the village continue over the hill into the next valley, then, at a right-hand bend just past the village hall, fork left onto a stony track leaving the D´Arcy Dalton Way. By two prominent trees fork left again over a stile and take path SM149a diagonally across a field, heading just right of a single wooden pylon right of a double pylon, to cross a stile just over the skyline. Now turn left onto bridleway SM149 following a left-hand hedge to a field corner where you turn right past a cottage garden to reach a bridlegate in the left-hand fence leading to the A423.

Cross this main road carefully and take bridleway SM149 straight on through a hedge gap opposite, passing through a gate into a field and following a right-hand hedge to a bridlegate at the far side. Now go straight on across the next field to reach a hedge gap just left of its far corner where superb panoramic views across three counties open out with Claydon immediately in front of you. Here go straight on downhill, aiming for the left-hand end of a shed in the valley bottom, to reach a gate on a rough road. Go through this and follow the rough road across two fields to a gate, then go through this and keep straight on across a railway level crossing with white bridlegates on the Oxford & Birmingham Railway. Now take a rough road straight on uphill towards Claydon. After 250 yards turn right over high rails opposite a gate onto path CC5, soon bearing slightly left and aiming just right of a modern barn on the hillside, crossing a low sheep-wire fence, then a ditch and a second fence and continuing to a gate near the barn. (NB If there is no footbridge and stile at the ditch, follow the second fence to a gate which you can climb over to rejoin the official line of the path at the gate near the barn). Now take a farm road straight on, bearing slightly right, then where it bears right, go straight on over a stile to reach a road onto which you turn left for your starting point.

Circular Walk No. 2   Horley

Length of Walk: (A) 5.3 miles / 8.6 Km
                 (B) 4.8 miles / 7.7 Km
Starting Point: Road junction by 'Red Lion`, Horley.
Grid Ref: SP418438
Maps: OS Landranger Sheet 151
          OS Explorer Sheet 206
          OS Pathfinder Sheets 1021 (SP24/34) & 1022
          (SP44/54)

How to get there / Parking: Horley, 3 miles northwest of
     Banbury, may be reached from the town centre by taking
     the A422 towards Wroxton. Before leaving the town,
     where the A422 turns left, take the B4100 straight on
     towards Warmington. After 1.5 miles turn left onto a road
     signposted to Horley and Hornton. On reaching Horley,
     at a road junction by the 'Red Lion`, bear left towards
     Wroxton and Shutford, then turn immediately left again
     into Gullivers Close where you can park.

Notes: While Walk A involves less road walking, bridleway
     HL1a on it can become heavily overgrown with nettles in
     the summer months and so Walk B is included to enable
     you to bypass this problem.

Horley, an attractive quiet hillside village with ironstone cottages, is in the midst of the area once used for quarrying this reddish stone for which neighbouring Hornton is particularly well known. The village has a fine Norman church, considerably altered and extended in the fourteenth century when its tower was built and noted for its large fifteenth-century wall painting of St. Christopher.

Both walks lead you northwestwards from Horley to join the D'Arcy Dalton Way and follow it to Bush Hill with its superb views across the remote Sor Brook valley towards Edge Hill in Warwickshire, scene in 1642 of the first major battle of the Civil War, before turning south to reach the picturesque village of Hornton. You then leave the D'Arcy Dalton Way and return by a pleasant direct route along the contours of the hillside on which both villages are situated.

Both walks start from the road junction by the ´Red Lion` in Horley and take the Hornton and Edge Hill road climbing past the church to your left and out of the village. By the village name-board ignore a drive to your right, then some 250 yards further on **Walk A** turns right onto bridleway HL1a and follows this rather overgrown lane for 300 yards to its end. Now turn left over a stile onto path HL1 bearing slightly right across two fields, crossing a slight rise in the first field and two stiles left of a gate in the far hedge of the second field. Here bear slightly left across the next field, gradually diverging from the right-hand hedge and passing left of a hedge corner left of an oak tree to reach a fence gap left of another tree. Now follow a right-hand hedge, wiggling right at one point, to cross a stile at the far end of the field, then continue to follow the hedge through a second field to a stile. Here bear half right heading towards a stile and footbridge in the far corner of the field. Before reaching them, level with a gap in the right-hand hedge, turn sharp left onto path HL18 joining the D´Arcy Dalton Way and heading for a corner of a fence by some hawthorn bushes. Now bear half right briefly joining the fence. Where the fence bears right again, leave it and go straight on uphill to a gate in a corner of the field. Here bear half left onto a macadam farm road and follow it uphill to Glebe Farm where you turn right between a barn and a diesel tank onto path HL2 rejoining Walk B.

Walk B ignores bridleway HL1a and continues along the road for a further third of a mile passing a large barn. Now, at a left-hand bend, fork right onto path HL2, following the back of the roadside hedge to a clump of trees, then bear slightly right across the field to cross a stile in the far hedge. Now go straight on across a large field, heading just right of the farmhouse and a twin-poled pylon at Glebe Farm, eventually crossing two wooden fences, a drive and two stiles to reach a lawn. Bear slightly left across this to a junction of drives, then go straight on through a concealed gate in a fence to reach a farmyard. Bear half right across this to pass left of a diesel tank and join the D´Arcy Dalton Way and Walk A.

Walks A and B now take path HL2 passing right of a barn and following a rough track. Where this turns left through a hedge gap, go straight on over a stile and follow a left-hand hedge with fine views to your right. About 100 yards short of the far end of the field at a slight kink in the hedge by Horley Fields Farm to your left, cross a stile and follow the other side of the hedge to a field corner. Here cross a stile and turn left following a left-hand hedge to a gap in the next hedge, then cross a track and bear half right across the next field with fine views to your right to reach a gap just left of the far corner. Go through this and take path HT10 straight on across the next field to a stile in the far hedge at Bush Hill where superb panoramic views open out across the Sor Brook valley towards Edge Hill ahead and Shotteswell on a hilltop to your right.

Here turn left onto fenced cart-track HT9 and follow it straight on for half a mile, soon with a fine view to your left towards Northamptonshire, ignoring a crossing track leading to a farm to your right. On reaching the Horley-Upton road, cross it and take path HT9 straight on over a stile following a left-hand fence to cross a second stile. Here bear slightly right across the next field to pass just right of two sycamore trees and cross a stile behind them, then follow a right-hand hedge downhill going through a gate, then pass right of a stone wall and a cottage and go through its gates and down its drive to reach a road in Hornton called Eastgate.

Hornton, with its attractive village green in a sheltered valley, is appropriately another village of fine ironstone cottages, as it is renowned for its building stone used in the construction of Liverpool Cathedral as well as many of the older houses in Banbury. Though still known as Hornton stone, it is no longer quarried in the village but instead at nearby Edge Hill, just over the Warwickshire border. In addition, the village can also boast a twelfth-century church noted for its late fourteenth-century wall-painting of the Last Judgement over its chancel arch.

Continue down Eastgate to the green, then turn left into Pages Lane. At its end take path HT2 straight on between cottages to cross a stile, then take path HT2a straight on across a field to a stile in its far right-hand corner. Now go straight on to the far left-hand corner of the next field with a fine view of an attractive lake opening out ahead. Here cross a stile and bear right, heading for the point where a left-hand fence meets a hedge at the left-hand end of the lake, to cross two stiles. Now take path HL7 straight on through this thick hedge, then follow a left-hand hedge straight on through two fields. At the far end of the second field go through a gate and bear slightly right to cross two stiles and a footbridge in a dip, then bear half right uphill to a stile into Clump Lane (bridleway HL6). Turn left into this lane and follow it uphill for 130 yards, then turn right over a stile and take the continuation of path HL7 bearing half left to the far end of a hedge. Here bear half left again, heading towards the fourth house right of Horley Church, eventually reaching a gate in the bottom hedge. Now follow a left-hand hedge through a scrubby field, a plantation and a grass field to a stile into a fenced path leading to a road in Horley where you turn right, descending to a T-junction near your starting point.

86

CIRCULAR WALK NO.2

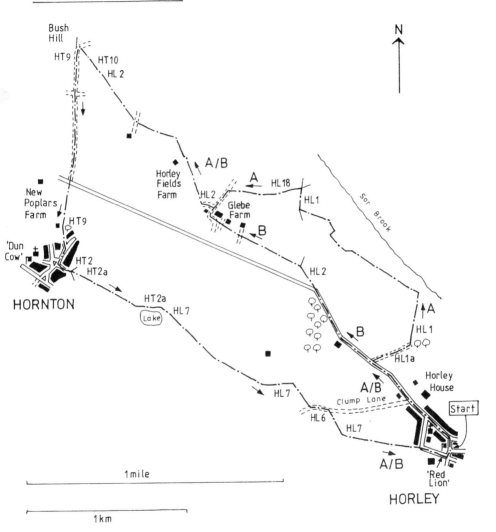

Circular Walk No. 3   Hook Norton

Length of Walk: 7.7 miles / 12.4 Km
Starting Point: ´Pear Tree Inn`, Scotland End, Hook Norton
Grid Ref: SP351332
Maps: OS Landranger Sheet 151
        OS Explorer Sheet 191
        OS Pathfinder Sheet 1044 (SP23/33)
How to get there / Parking: Hook Norton, 8 miles southwest
of Banbury, may be reached from the town by taking the
A361 towards Chipping Norton for 4 miles. After going
through Bloxham, turn right onto the Milcombe, Wigginton and Hook Norton road and follow it for 4 miles to
Hook Norton. In the village take the winding priority
road to the far end known as Scotland End. Where the
road forks by a small green, turn right onto the Sibford
Gower road and park immediately on your right. If no
space is available here, continue along the road and seek
a suitable parking place. Do not use the car park of the
´Pear Tree Inn` without the landlord´s permission.

Hook Norton, locally called ´Hookey` and scene in 914 A.D. of a
bloody battle with the invading Danes, is now best known for its
brewery. One of the smallest surviving breweries in Britain, it
was founded by John Harris in 1849 and its architecturally fascinating buildings date from 1899. As recently as 1945, Hook
Norton was a hive of industry with, as well as the brewery, the
Brymbo Ironworks, active ironstone quarries and the Banbury-Cheltenham railway built in 1887 crossing the valley on an
80-foot high viaduct. However today the ironworks and railway
have closed and the pillars of the viaduct and quarry faces are
rapidly disappearing beneath rampant tree cover, so that this
large Redland village in its quiet valley with a wealth of fine stone
cottages dominated by the impressive Perpendicular tower of its
originally Norman church, when seen from the surrounding hills,
appears to have descended into an enchanted slumber.

The walk starts from this last ironstone village on the D´Arcy
Dalton Way and follows the Way up South Hill with its fine views
back across the village and along its remote highest section to
Great Rollright, the first of the Cotswold-stone villages on the

Way. From here you leave the Way and turn north into Warwickshire with more fine views across the remote hills around Whichford before descending into Ascott and turning east over Whichford Hill to reach Hook Norton by the brewery.

Starting from the green by the ´Pear Tree Inn`, take the Great Rollright and Chipping Norton road over a bridge over a stream. Now turn left over a stile by a gate onto path HN3 following a left-hand tree-belt along the field edge. Near the far end of the field ignore a gate to your left and take path HN2 crossing two stiles in the field corner, then bear half right across a field to a stile in the far corner right of a line of bungalows leading to Croft´s Lane. Turn left onto this road then, after 30 yards, turn right through a gate onto path HN1 and the D´Arcy Dalton Way. (NB It is currently not possible to walk the definitive line of this path due to obstructions and so the de facto line is described. If you find another line waymarked, it would be advisable to follow it as it probably means that the path has been restored to its definitive line.) Bear slightly left to a second gate then half right across a field to a gate left of an electricity pole. Now go straight on across the next field to cross two rail-stiles, then continue across a further field to a gate and rail-stile into a green lane. Turn left down this lane to a stile by a gate and farm-bridge in the valley bottom then bear slightly right up the next field to a gap left of a tall ash tree. Now bear half right to cross rails by a gate left of a clump of ash trees then bear half right across a further field, where there are fine views over Hook Norton behind you, to reach a hedge gap at the right-hand end of a line of trees leading to the road at South Hill.

Turn right onto this road and follow it gently downhill. After 250 yards, at the far end of a row of conifers to your left, turn left onto path HN6, the drive to Fanville Farm, and follow it straight on passing a fine modern timbered house to your left and ignoring all branching tracks and drives. At the far side of the farm go through a gate and take path HN5 straight on, disregarding all gates and branching tracks to left and right and eventually emerging into a left-hand field. Here take a shallow sunken way straight on beside the right-hand hedge, soon becoming enclosed by a left-hand hedge. On reemerging into the field, the sunken way soon peters out. Where the right-hand hedge bears away to the right, leave it and go straight on across the field to a gap in the next hedge, then bear slightly left across the field beyond with views behind you towards the Sibfords to reach a hedge gap just right of a stunted oak tree on the skyline, the highest point on the D´Arcy Dalton

Way at approximately 221 metres or 725 feet above sea level.

Go through this gap crossing a grassy track then take path RR1 bearing half right across the next field heading just right of a tall sycamore tree in a distant hedge to cross an unclassified road and stone stile in a stone wall. Now bear slightly right across a further field to a gap in a stone wall by a clump of bushes. Here bear half right across a corner of the next field to a hedge gap by the tall sycamore tree where Great Rollright Church comes into view ahead. Now bear slightly right across a further field heading towards a modern barn at Church End Farm right of the church to a rail-stile in the next hedge. Cross this and bear slightly left down-hill to cross a footbridge in the valley bottom then bear half left uphill, heading for the church when it comes into view, to cross a stile in the top corner of the field leading to a road. Cross the road and go through a gate opposite into Great Rollright Churchyard then bear half left across the churchyard passing left of the church to reach the lychgate leading to a road known as Church End.

Great Rollright, as immediately becomes obvious on seeing its church, is the first Cotswold limestone village on the D´Arcy Dalton Way. This twelfth-century church with a fifteenth-century tower, though ancient in itself, however, in no way, marks the foundation of the village as Great Rollright is mentioned in the Domesday Book of 1086 and its location on a road thought to be the most ancient in Britain, possibly dating back to the Stone Age, suggests that habitation of this site may go back a long way further.

Take Church End soon bearing right, then at a road junction go straight on. At a right-hand bend fork left through a kissing-gate onto path RR13 heading for a gap in the houses at the far corner of the field. About halfway across, fork right onto path RR12 crossing a stile at the corner of a hedge then pass right of some garages to join a residential road onto which you turn right then left to reach a T-junction. Here turn right, then at a crossroads, leaving the D´Arcy Dalton Way, take the Whichford and Banbury road straight on for a quarter mile to the next junction. Now fork left through a gate onto path RR11 bearing slightly right across the first field to a gate and stile, then half left across the second to a rail-stile in the far corner. Cross this, a farm road and a second rail-stile, then bear half left across a field to the right-hand corner of a farm compound. Here go straight on towards the top of a tall ash tree on the skyline, now with a fine view towards Brailes Hill ahead. On nearing the ash tree, turn right to follow a left-hand fence then a hedge to the far end of the field where you cross a stile at the Warwickshire boundary. Now take path SS82 straight on through two fields with fine views to

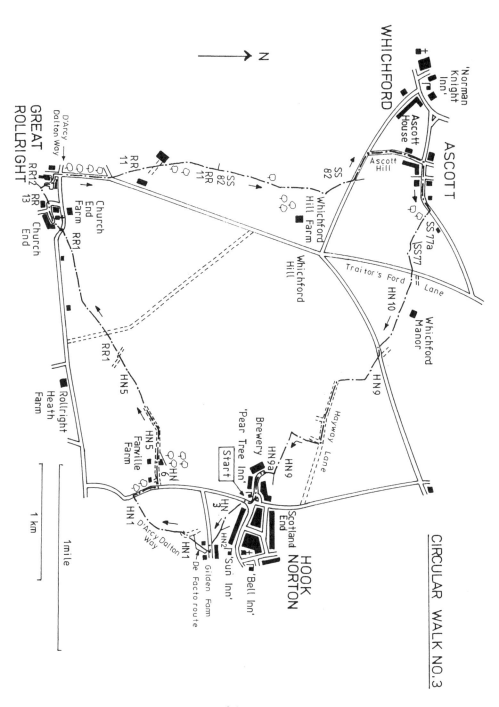

CIRCULAR WALK NO.3

91

your left across the Long Compton valley, walking parallel to the left-hand hedge in the first, then passing just left of the farthest right of the midfield ash trees in the second to cross a stile in the far hedge. Here follow the left-hand hedge, later a ditch straight on through a third field then go through a hedge gap, crossing an old gate and a stile into a fourth field. Now turn left beside a left-hand hedge, later a fence to reach a flight of steps and a stile in the roadside hedge to your right. At the top of the steps turn left onto the Whichford road for 250 yards to a road junction, then turn right onto the road signposted to Ascott, soon descending Ascott Hill to the crossroads in the centre of the hamlet.

Here turn right and ignoring a branching road to your left, go straight on out of Ascott. 150 yards beyond a left-hand bend turn right over a stile onto path SS77a following a right-hand hedge steeply uphill, soon passing a copse to cross a stile in the top hedge, then bear half left across a field with fine views opening out behind you, to reach a kink in the left-hand hedge 150 yards short of the far corner. Here, joining bridleway SS77, turn left through a bridle-gate in the hedge and bear half right across the top of a steeply sloping field to join a right-hand fence and follow it to a corner. Now go through a gate and continue beside a left-hand hedge to a gate onto Traitor's Ford Lane at the Oxfordshire boundary.

Ignore a farm road opposite and take bridleway HN10 through a hedge gap just right of it beside a left-hand hedge for half a mile, soon with a fine view across the Stour valley towards the Sibfords through a hedge gap to your left, to reach a hedge gap onto Oatley Hill. Turn left onto this road and after 80 yards opposite the drive to Whichford Manor turn right through a gap onto path HN9 bearing half left across a field to cross a stile under a willow tree. Now follow a left-hand hedge for 300 yards to gates in the hedge. Turn left through these and take a grassy track by a right-hand hedge through two fields to a gate and stile into Hayway Lane. After 130 yards at a junction of farm roads, turn right over a stile and follow a right-hand hedge with Hook Norton Brewery coming into view to your left and views towards Whichford Hill in places to your right. At the far side of the field go through a hunting gate then bear half left across a narrow field aiming between Hook Norton Church and the brewery to reach a hedge gap in the far corner of the field. Now follow a right-hand hedge, then, where it bears right, turn right over a stile by a gate onto path HN9a and follow a left-hand hedge to a gate and stile by the brewery. Here take Brewery Lane bearing left past the brewery, ignoring a branching road to the left and continuing to the 'Pear Tree Inn`.

Circular Walk No. 4   Salford (Oxon.)

Length of Walk: 4.0 miles / 6.4 Km
Starting Point: Crossroads on Salford village green.
Grid Ref: SP290282
Maps: OS Landranger Sheets 151 & 164
OS Outdoor Leisure Sheet 45 & Explorer Sheet 191
OS Pathfinder Sheets 1044 (SP23/33) & 1068 (SP22/32)
How to get there / Parking: Salford, 1.6 miles northwest of Chipping Norton, may be reached from the town by taking the A44 towards Evesham for 1.8 miles then taking the first turning right into Salford. At a T-junction by the ´Black Horse` turn right then bear left and follow the main village street to a green where the road widens out by a children´s playground and it is possible to park.

Salford, in a hollow just off the A44, bears little resemblance to its more famous northern namesake, the home of ´Coronation Street`. The name of both is, in fact, probably a corruption of ´salt-ford` and, in the case of the Oxfordshire village, results from its proximity to the A44, part of the old London-Worcester turnpike road and an ancient ´salt-track` used for transporting the salt from salt-mines in the Midlands to London, essential to the storage of meat in the days  before the discovery of electricity and invention of the freezer. The village, though suffering from modern ´infilling,` can boast some picturesque Cotswold-stone cottages and a church of Norman origin, which was substantially rebuilt in the fourteenth century when its tower was added.

The walk leads you northeast from Salford along a quiet Cotswold valley climbing gently to meet the D´Arcy Dalton Way near Brighthill Farm. You then turn southwestwards onto the D´Arcy Dalton Way passing within sight of the fascinating prehistoric Rollright Stones and continuing with fine views past the equally fascinating deserted village of Little Rollright then dropping gradually back into Salford.

Starting from the crossroads on Salford village green, turn left into Golden Lane, the road to Rectory Farm and ignoring branching paths and drives, continue along an avenue of poplars (now on

93

CIRCULAR WALK NO. 4

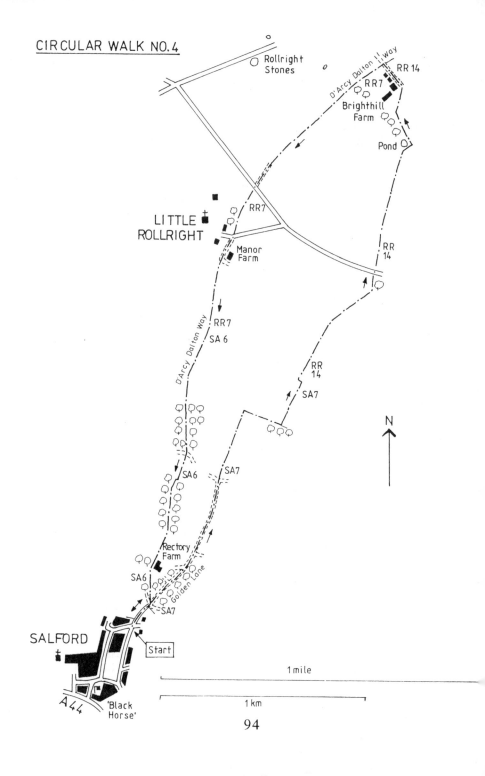

Rollright Stones

D'Arcy Dalton way

RR 14

RR 7

Brighthill Farm

Pond

LITTLE ROLLRIGHT

RR 7

Manor Farm

RR 14

D'Arcy Dalton way

RR 7
SA 6

RR 14
SA 7

N

SA 6

SA 7

Rectory Farm

SA 6

Golden Lane

SA 7

SALFORD

Start

A 44

'Black Horse'

1 mile

1 km

94

bridleway SA7). Disregard the entrance to Rectory Farm to your left, where the macadam surface ends, and continue for a third of a mile, soon with fine views of the surrounding hills in all directions, ignoring a branching track to your right. Where the track forks left and right, take a grassy bridleway straight on beside a right-hand hedge to a bridlegate into the next field, then turn right beside a right-hand hedge. 100 yards short of the far side of the field turn left across it to a gap in the far hedge then take bridleway RR14 bearing left into a field corner then right following a left-hand hedge to the far side of the field. Here cross a shallow ford and bear slightly right across the next field to join the left-hand edge of an area of trees concealing the site of Rollright Mill and follow it to reach a road which, despite its narrowness, was, till the construction of the modern A3400 in the 1820s, part of the Oxford - Stratford-upon-Avon turnpike road, by a fine old stone bridge.

Cross this road and take path RR14 bearing slightly left across a field to its far corner. Here ignore two large hedge gaps to your left and go straight on through a smaller one into the right-hand field. Now follow a left-hand hedge to the far end of the field where you turn right uphill for 50 yards to a stile. Turn left over this and follow a left-hand fence past an ornamental lake, then a left-hand hedge entering a young plantation to reach a stile. Now bear half right up the next field to a gate and stile right of Brighthill Farm then take a farm road uphill past the farm to a rail-stile in the left-hand fence on the crossing D´Arcy Dalton Way. Here turn left over two rail-stiles onto path RR7 and bear slightly right across a field to cross two further stiles at the right-hand end of a belt of tall trees, then go through a hedge gap with the Rollright Stones coming into view to your right and fine views opening out down the valley ahead towards Salford and the distant Evenlode valley and to your left towards the outskirts of Chipping Norton on a hillside.

The Rollright Stones, believed to date from sometime between 2000 B.C. and 1500 B.C., can be divided into three groups: the Whispering Knights, the remains of an ancient burial chamber, near the right-hand hedge of the field; the King´s Men, a circle of 77 stones of various sizes, in the far corner of the field and the King´s Stone, a single eight-foot-high stone on a low mound on the other side of the ridgetop road in Warwickshire. The names would seem to have little to do with the real origin of the stones but rather derive from a local legend that an ancient king, who was attempting to conquer England and was leading his army towards the crest of the Cotswold escarpment, was stopped by a witch who turned them to stone and herself into an elderbush; the King´s Stone being the king, the King's Men being his army and the Whispering Knights lagging behind and plotting against him. There is no public access to the Whispering Knights which can, indeed, best be seen from where you are on path RR7, while access to the King's Stone and King's Men is only available from the ridgetop road. If wishing to take a closer look at them, you should therefore continue along the D'Arcy Dalton Way to the next crossing road, then turn right onto this and turn right again at the next crossroads.

Now take path RR7 straight on across the field to a gap in the far hedge, then keep straight on beside a sporadic left-hand hedge entering a sunken way by an ash tree and following it downhill to a gate and gap onto the old turnpike road. Go through a hedge gap opposite where the largely deserted village of Little Rollright comes into view in its hollow ahead and bear slightly left down the field to the near left-hand corner of the 'lost village` site then bear half left across a field corner towards a twin-poled electricity pylon to reach the road into the village.

Unlike many Oxfordshire 'lost villages,` which became depopulated due to the ravages of the Black Death or agricultural malpractice impoverishing the soil, Little Rollright was reduced to a church, a manor house and a scattering of remote farms and cottages by early inclosure in about 1500 which resulted in the forcible eviction of most of its population. Despite the fact that this deprived the tiny fifteenth-century church of most of its congregation, William Blower in 1617 extended the church by giving it its pinnacled tower and it has only survived thanks to the generosity of various benefactors who have ensured its upkeep.

Now take path RR7 straight on across the road and down a farm road into the yard of Manor Farm. Here keep straight on between barns to a hedge gap into a field, then climb this field to a stile in its top hedge. Now take path SA6 following a right-hand hedge straight on with a fine view to your left towards Chipping Norton. At the far end of the field go through a hunting-gate and downhill through a plantation. At its far side cross a track and go through a shallow ford then follow a right-hand hedge for 120 yards to reach gates in it. Go through these and follow the other side of the hedge to a gate into another plantation. Take the obvious path through it, then cross a stile into a field and bear slightly left across it to a corner of a hedge surrounding Rectory Farm. Now follow this hedge straight on to cross a stile in a corner of the field, then bear slightly left to cross a second stile where you bear half left across a field to a stile in its far corner leading to Golden Lane on the edge of Salford, where you turn right for your starting point.

Circular Walk No. 5   Ascott-under-Wychwood

Length of Walk: 8.7 miles / 14.0 Km
Starting Point: Ascott-under-Wychwood village green.
Grid Ref: SP302188
Maps: OS Landranger Sheets 163 & 164
        OS Outdoor Leisure Sheet 45 & Explorer
        Sheets 180 & 191
        OS Pathfinder Sheets 1068 (SP22/32) &
        1091 (SP21/31)
How to get there / Parking: Ascott-under-Wychwood, 5 miles
south of Chipping Norton, may be reached from the town
by taking the A361 towards Burford for 4.8 miles then
turning left onto the Ascott-under-Wychwood road and
following it downhill into the village. Having crossed a
level-crossing by Ascott-under-Wychwood Station, ignore
the first turning right then, at The Green, turn right and
park immediately on your right.

Ascott-under-Wychwood with its attractive stone cottages, like
the other two villages sharing the appendage ´under-Wychwood`,
is situated in the Evenlode valley below the ridge separating the
Evenlode and Windrush valleys, much of which was covered
until the 1850s by the ancient royal forest of Wychwood. The
present village was, in fact, originally three separate hamlets: one
around the Norman church and two others known as Ascott
d´Oyley and Ascott Earl, each of which was built around a
twelfth-century castle, but the opening of the Oxford, Worcester
and Wolverhampton Railway in 1853 (locally nicknamed ´The
Old Worse and Worse`) caused the village to expand so that the
separate hamlets have now merged. Neither of the castles has
survived, but the manor house built by Sir William Jones in 1620
is situated within the bailey of the Ascott d´Oyley Castle and
incorporates some mediæval buttresses and mullioned windows
from the castle. It also boasts a seventeenth-century barn with a
dovecot in the gable and a brick and half-timber granary built
on staddle stones.

The walk, which has many fine views and includes substantial

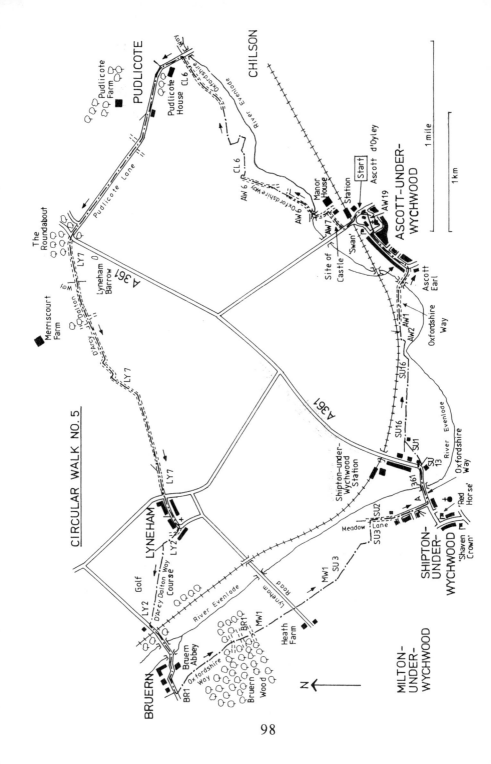

CIRCULAR WALK NO. 5

98

sections of both the D´Arcy Dalton Way and the Oxfordshire Way, leads you from Ascott-under-Wychwood down the Evenlode valley to the deserted village of Pudlicote before climbing to the top of the ridge above Lyneham where there are ancient earthworks and superb views across the upper Evenlode valley. You then descend to Lyneham and Bruern with its abbey and return down the valley by way of Shipton-under-Wychwood with its fine Cotswold-stone church and houses to reach Ascott.

Starting from the northern corner of The Green in Ascott-under-Wychwood, take the Chipping Norton road northwards crossing the railway level-crossing by Ascott-under-Wychwood Station, then at a left-hand bend turn right onto path AW7 following the drive to Manor Farm and looking out for the earthworks of Ascott d´Oyley Castle in the adjacent fields. Where the drive bears right by a stone barn, turn left onto a fenced grassy track and follow it to cross a bridge over the River Evenlode. Now take the track bearing right, joining bridleway AW6, part of the northern route of the Oxfordshire Way, and continuing with fine views of the Evenlode valley including some of the woods remaining from the ancient Wychwood Forest on the hills to your right, keeping left of a hedge to reach a gate at the far end of the field. Go through this and bear slightly right across the next field to join a right-hand hedge where it bulges out. At the far end of the field bear right through a gate by a willow tree and take bridleway CL6 turning right and following a willow-lined tributary of the Evenlode to the far end of the field. Here turn left and follow a right-hand hedge, soon bearing left then right to reach the second gate in it. Turn right over a stile by this gate and now with more open views along and across the Evenlode valley including the small village of Chilson to your right, go straight across the field heading for the right-hand end of a copse and derelict barn to reach a gate and stile. Now follow a grassy track beside a left-hand hedge to a gated culvert where Pudlicote House comes into view ahead. Here take a grassy track bearing half right across a parkland field, with the deserted village of Shorthampton coming into view on a rise ahead and a closer view of Chilson to your right, to reach a gate and bridlegate, then continue along a fenced track to a gate onto Pudlicote Lane.

Leaving the Oxfordshire Way, turn left onto this quiet road and follow it gently uphill for over a mile with pleasant views virtually throughout, passing Pudlicote´s scattered dwellings, then with superb views up the Evenlode valley opening out to your left by Pudlicote Farm, with Ascott-under-Wychwood in the foreground and the spire of Leafield´s Victorian church on the skyline. Near the top of the ridge ignore the Chadlington road to your right, then at a T-junction with the A361 in a wood known as The Roundabout as there is a circular earthwork concealed by trees on the other side of the main road thought to be an ancient cattle pound, cross the A361 and take bridleway LY7 through a gap by a gate opposite. Now follow a farm track along the edge of the wood then beside a right-hand hedge, generally descending gently for 1.2 miles with superb views ahead across the upper Evenlode valley including Milton-under-Wychwood, Lyneham, Fifield, Idbury, Kingham and Stow-on-the-Wold and joining the D´Arcy Dalton Way in the second field where Merriscourt Farm comes into view to your right. In the third field you ignore a branching green lane to your right, then in the fifth you disregard a branching track and eventually enter a green lane which becomes a macadam road and leads you to a crossroads in Lyneham.

Lyneham in the Evenlode valley is a small attractive Cotswold village, most of which flanks the street you are about to walk. Traditionally a hamlet of Shipton-under-Wychwood, Lyneham only became an independent parish in modern times.

Here cross the major road and go straight on down the village street. Where it eventually turns left, turn right onto path LY2 along a gravel lane. Just past the last left-hand cottage where the track bears right, leave it and follow a left-hand stone wall to cross a footbridge onto a golf course. Here go straight on, passing left of a bunker to go through a hedge gap, then bear half left keeping just left of a green, a raised tee, a small bunker at the far side of the next fairway and another green to cross a culvert by an oak tree. Now head for a five-bar gate between the level crossing gates and the former crossing-keeper´s cottage at Bruern Crossing, passing right of a green and a pond to cross a stile by the gate onto a road.

Bruern, which for walkers is significant as the crossing point of the D´Arcy Dalton Way and Oxfordshire Way, comprises little more than Bruern Abbey and a few cottages on a road leading to bridges over the Evenlode. The present Bruern Abbey, built by the Cope family in the early eighteenth century on the site of a Cistercian abbey founded in 1147, was home to Sir John Cope, commander-in-chief of forces in Scotland at the time of the 1745 rebellion. Although his forces were routed by Bonny Prince Charlie at Prestonpans, Cope was not blamed for this defeat and a year later the rebellion was crushed at the Battle of Culloden.

Turn left onto the road, crossing the railway and bridges over various courses of the Evenlode, then continue past the grounds of

Bruern Abbey and a few cottages. On leaving the village, a view of Bruern Abbey opens out over your left shoulder, then, on reaching the crossing Oxfordshire Way, you turn left through a bridlegate onto bridleway BR1 bearing half left across a parkland field with more views of Bruern Abbey to your left to reach the corner of a fence. Here bear half right passing left of a fenced football field, then go through gates and continue across a field to a small hedge gap into Bruern Wood. In the wood take a wide firebreak straight on across it. At its far side bear half left through a concealed bridlegate and take bridleway MW1 following a right-hand hedge with fine views ahead down the Evenlode valley towards Wychwood Forest and to your left across the valley towards Lyneham, to reach a bridlegate into a fenced bridleway leading to Lyneham Road.

Cross this road and take fenced bridleway MW1 straight on to a gate and stile into a field then bear slightly right crossing two fields with Shipton-under-Wychwood beginning to come into view ahead. At the far side of the second field cross a stile by a gate and take bridleway SU3 along what is normally a grass crop-break with wider views across Shipton-under-Wychwood opening out ahead, eventually bearing right to reach the corner of a hedge. Here turn left and follow a right-hand hedge to reach a hedge gap leading into Meadow Lane (bridleway SU2). Turn right into this lane which soon becomes surfaced and continue until you reach the A361 on the edge of Shipton-under-Wychwood.

Shipton-under-Wychwood, a large village at the point where the Evenlode turns northeast around the Wychwood ridge, gives the immediate impression of mediæval wealth when the tall spire of its twelfth-century church comes into view in the distance. The name 'Shipton' meaning 'sheep farm', indeed, points to the source of Cotswold prosperity in the Middle Ages, namely the wool trade. This was no doubt supplemented by the village forming the centre of a royal estate including the ancient royal forest of Wychwood. In addition to its church, Shipton, which was home to the fourteenth-century poet William Langland, can also boast numerous other buildings of interest including the tastefully renovated fifteenth-century 'Shaven Crown', which derives its name from its links with the monks of Bruern Abbey, and Shipton Court, which was remodelled by the Laceys in 1603 but may be much older. Finally, on the green there is a fountain in memory of seventeen former residents who drowned when the 'Cospatrick', which was taking them to a new life in New Zealand, caught fire and sank off Tristan da Cunha in 1874.

Turn left along the footway of the A361 crossing a bridge over the Evenlode, then at a left-hand bend just past a filling station, turn right crossing the road and taking path SU1 through two sets of gates then bearing half left across a field to pass left of a ruined stone building and cross a double stile behind it. Here turn right onto path SU16 following a right-hand hedge. Where the hedge ends, continue along the edge of cultivation to join another right-hand hedge and follow it to the railway fence. Here turn right onto path AW2 entering a belt of scrub and continuing through it to a stile, then bear slightly right across a scrubby field to cross a footbridge. Now turn left and follow the left-hand ditch to rejoin the railway fence and reach a gated railway crossing. Here do not cross the railway, but take bridleway AW1 straight on to a gate into a green lane, then follow the green lane, eventually bearing right, crossing a bridge over the Evenlode and joining a macadam drive to reach a bend in Shipton Road at Ascott Earl.

Turn left onto this road and follow it for a quarter mile, soon passing the site of the twelfth-century castle. Just before reaching the ´Swan`, turn right into Church View, immediately forking left through a kissing-gate into Ascott churchyard and taking path AW19 along a fine avenue of lime trees passing the church to your right to reach gates into Church Close which leads you back to the village green.

Circular Walk No. 6   Langford

Length of Walk: (A) 13.4 miles / 21.6 Km
(B) 13.1 miles / 21.1 Km
Starting Point: Gates to Langford Church.
Grid Ref: SP250025
Maps: OS Landranger Sheet 163
OS Outdoor Leisure Sheet 45 & Explorer Sheet 170
OS Pathfinder Sheets 1115 (SP20/30) &
1135 (SU29/39)

How to get there / Parking: Langford, 8 miles southwest of
Witney, may be reached from the town by taking the
A4095 towards Faringdon for 8 miles. Having passed
through Clanfield, turn right onto the road to Grafton,
Langford and Kelmscot. After two-thirds of a mile turn
right again onto the Grafton and Langford road. In
Langford park either in the bay opposite the church or
others near the ´Bell Inn`, but do not use the pub car park
without the landlord´s permission.

Notes: It is inadvisable to attempt the walk when the River
Thames is in flood as parts of it may be under water.

Langford, until the nineteenth century a detached parish of
Berkshire, is a remote and attractive stone-built Cotswold-style
village in the Upper Thames plain near the Gloucestershire
border. Apart from its fine stone cottages, Langford´s principal
attraction is its church, one of the few in the county of Saxon
origin to survive. Though much altered by the Normans and with
aisles added and its chancel rebuilt in the thirteenth century, the
church retains its Saxon central tower (albeit with a late Norman
parapet) and a Saxon south porch and sundial, but perhaps its
greatest treasure is the Langford Rood, a rare example of Saxon
sculpture.

The walks which, though relatively long, are easy in nature
being virtually flat throughout, lead you northeast from
Langford to join the D´Arcy Dalton Way and follow it southeast-
wards to meet the Thames. You then follow the Thames Path
westwards almost to Lechlade with Walk A taking a detour to
visit Kelmscot, William Morris´s ´heaven on earth`, before
turning northeast to return to Langford. Despite its flatness, this

103

walk is in no way monotonous as it passes a number of places of interest and offers a series of fine views both of the river and across its valley towards the surrounding hills.

Both walks start from the gates to Langford Church and take the road into the village. Before reaching the ´Bell Inn`, turn right by a telephone box onto path LA11 along a green lane. At the end of the lane cross a stile by a gate and follow a right-hand hedge through two fields to a footbridge with stiles. Cross these and take path BW8 bearing slightly left across a field to a gap in the next hedge, then follow a left-hand hedge straight on to a stile into Calcroft Lane. Now continue through a squeeze-stile opposite and bear slightly right across a field to a gap in the far hedge, then go straight across another field to a footbridge in the next hedge and bear slightly left across a third, with views of Broadwell´s massive thirteenth-century church spire to your left, to a squeeze-stile and footbridge in the next hedge. Now, joining the D´Arcy Dalton Way, take path BW7 bearing right across a further field to a stile and footbridge over Langhat Ditch under a willow tree in the middle of the far hedge. Cross these and a further stile, then take path AV19 bearing half right across the next field to the right-hand corner of a copse where you bear right joining path AV14 to cross a stile by a gate just right of Lower Rookshill Farm. Now take a farm road straight on beside a left-hand hedge for a third of a mile to reach a T-junction of farm roads by a bridge carrying Calcroft Lane over the former East Gloucestershire Railway from Oxford to Fairford, built in 1873 and closed by Dr. Beeching in 1962 and locally known as the ´Fairford Flyer`. Here turn right and follow a farm road to a gate and stile onto Calcroft Lane.

Turn right onto this road and after 40 yards turn left over a stile onto path BW12 bearing slightly left across a field to a stile onto the old railway (now a farm road). Cross these and take path BW12a straight on across a large field to reach the corner of a hedge by a hedge gap. Do **not** go through this gap, but follow the left-hand hedge straight on for a quarter mile with views towards Coleshill to your right, looking out for a footbridge and stiles in the hedge. Turn left over these then right and take path CF10 following the hedge and stream at first. Where these bear right, leave them and bear slightly right across the field to pass through a gate by an ash tree, then turn left and follow a left-hand hedge to go through another gate. Now bear slightly right across the next field heading towards a farm at Little Clanfield to pass through a gate in the next hedge, then keep straight on, heading between the farm and a stone cottage, crossing a stile and reaching a road at Little Clanfield.

Little Clanfield, at the end of a mile-long cul-de-sac lane, is today, like its near neighbour Grafton, a collection of scattered farms and cottages, but pre-inclosure maps suggest that both hamlets were once larger and that inclosure in the 1830s and 1840s may have caused or contributed to their depopulation.

Cross this road and take path CF9 straight on through a hedge gap and beside a right-hand willow copse. At the far end of the copse, turn right and follow the winding field edge until, near the far side of the field, you reach a footbridge to your right. Turn right over this and take path CF14 bearing slightly left across a large field, passing just right of the first wooden electricity pylon then left of a line of four to reach a hedge gap leading to a green lane. Continue along this, passing a cottage to your right, then soon joining a farm road which you follow straight on to reach Langley Lane.

Turn left into Langley Lane, then, after 30 yards, turn right onto path CF11, following a concrete road for a third of a mile, which bears left (becoming path GR1) and continues to Radcot Bridge Farm. Here bear half left onto a gravel track passing left of the farm and joining a right-hand hedge. At a field corner go straight on through a hedge gap and over a culvert, then leave the track and bear half left across a large field with views of Folly Hill, Faringdon to your right, passing just left of a wooden pylon, ignoring a crossing bridleway in mid-field and continuing until you reach a farm road just right of the far corner of the field. Turn left onto this then right through a gate and over a culvert. Here turn left over a stile and bear half right, disregarding a gated culvert to your left but noticing the earthworks to which it leads, known as ´The Garrison` believed to be a camp created by Prince Rupert in 1645 in his defence of Radcot Bridge against Parliamentary forces. Now continue to a footbridge on the Thames Path on the edge of Radcot where the ´Swan Hotel` is to your left.

Radcot, on the A4095 Witney - Faringdon road, has been the site of a bridge across the Thames for over 1000 years, as a Saxon chronicle refers to one already in existence in 958A.D. Since 1787, however, when attempts were made to improve the navigability of the Upper Thames by digging a new channel, there have been two bridges at Radcot, the more northerly one dating from that year, while the more southerly one, believed to be the oldest surviving bridge on the Thames, is thought to date from the thirteenth century. As one of the few bridges over the Thames in mediæval times, Radcot Bridge was of strategic importance and in 1387 the rebellious Henry Bolingbroke demolished its central arch in order to cut off Richard II's forces under the Earl of Oxford, who were subsequently routed, while during the Civil War it was the scene of a series of skirmishes between 1644 and 1646 before ultimately succumbing to Parliamentary control. Both bridges, which are said to be haunted by the ghost of a boatman beheaded by a local farmer whose sheep he stole, are built of Taynton stone and the gardens of the 'Swan Inn' mark the site of a wharf where this stone was loaded for use further downstream, while nearby is a seventeenth-century manor house.

Here do **not** cross the footbridge, but turn right onto the Thames Path (GR6) and follow it upstream passing the first of a number of Second World War 'pillboxes' or anti-aircraft gun emplacements you will see in the second field. After half a mile at a right-hand bend in the river there are views to your left of an old windpump and Folly Hill, then after another half mile you pass Grafton Lock (formerly known as Day's Weir or Lower Hart's Weir) which is notable for its superbly-kept flowerbeds. Soon on path KM3, after a further three-quarters of a mile you pass the scattered community of Eaton Hastings with its compact Norman church on the opposite bank, then, after a further two-thirds of a mile, you pass through a kissing-gate and small car park on the edge of Kelmscot and follow a rough road until it leaves the river.

Kelmscot, a picturesque village with numerous fine stone-built houses and farm buildings with slate roofs, is best known for its Elizabethan manor house which was leased as a summer retreat by the pre-Raphaelite designer, interior decorator, writer and printer, William Morris and his friend and colleague Daniel Gabriel Rossetti in 1871. While Rossetti soon became bored with Kelmscot and relinquished his share of the lease, Morris, who adored its peace and tranquillity, retained it until his death in 1896 and is buried in the churchyard of the village's small cruciform twelfth-century church. After his death his widow had Philip Webb design some cottages for the village and in 1934 the Morris Memorial Hall was built by Ernest Gimson and opened by the playwright, George Bernard Shaw.

Here **Walk B** turns left over a footbridge and through a gate and takes the continuation of the Thames Path (KM3) along the riverbank past Kelmscot for half a mile to reach a handgate into scrub near a footbridge over the river where it rejoins Walk A, while **Walk A** continues along the rough road (now on path KM4) to reach the end of the village street by Kelmscot Manor. Here bear right along the village street, then go left at fork. At a second fork by the 'Plough Inn' bear right, then just past the inn, by the base of an old stone cross, fork left onto path KM1 passing through the pub car park and continuing along a green lane which bears right by some gates. At the end of the lane turn left and follow a left-hand hedge. At the far side of the field go straight on over two footbridges then bear slightly right and follow a right-hand fence to a handgate into scrub on the Thames Path (KM3) where you rejoin Walk B.

Walks A and B now take path KM3 through the scrub and keep right at a fork, **not** crossing the Thames footbridge at Hart's Weir. This was the site of the last flashlock on the navigable Thames which was removed in 1936 and was named after a former lock-keeper who, in the 1830s, is reputed to have hidden kegs of contraband spirits at the bottom of the river secured by long chains. Now continue along the Thames Path (KM3), after a field's length passing through two handgates to enter Gloucestershire. Now on path LL27, continue along the riverbank for a further mile, looking out for glimpses of distant Buscot Park to your left, (a stately home dating from about 1770 now owned by the National Trust) and eventually reaching a bridge over the weir stream at Buscot, newly created in 1979. Cross this bridge, then keep left, following the bank of the old river then the lock stream to Buscot Lock where Buscot village, a model village rebuilt in 1879 and now owned by the National Trust, can be reached by crossing the gates at the far end of the lock and taking paths BS11 and BS3.

Otherwise, by the gates at the far end of the lock turn right onto a macadam path (still LL27) crossing the weir, then, ignoring a stile and gate ahead, bearing left and following the fenced towpath for nearly a further mile with Lechlade Church, a striking fifteenth-century 'wool church' with a sixteenth-century tower and spire coming into view ahead and after a quarter mile passing Buscot Church to your left. Buscot Church dates from about 1200 and has a fifteenth-century tower and is notable for its early sixteenth-century pulpit-panels painted by the Flemish artist Jan Gossaert, known as Mabuse, and its east window by the Pre-Raphaelite artist and friend of William Morris, Sir Edward Burne-Jones. Eventually, on rounding a large pool known as Bloomer's Hole where it is hoped that a footbridge will be built to take the Thames Path across to the south bank, take path LL27 turning right to cross a V-stile and continuing along a fenced track beside a line of poplars, eventually entering an avenue of trees to reach a road.

Turn left onto this road, crossing a bridge over the River Leach by the picturesque Priory Mill. Just past the mill turn right onto path LL18, ignoring a gate ahead and taking the fenced path to the right of it. Where the fenced path turns right and ends, go straight on over two stiles, then continue to a third in a hedge gap ahead. Now follow a right-hand hedge concealing the River Leach straight on to reach a stile leading into a factory yard where you follow the riverbank straight on to reach Mill Lane. Turn right onto this narrow road, crossing two bridges over arms of the River Leach and passing Lechlade Mill hidden to your left. After 150 yards by a tall cypress tree turn left onto path LL20, passing the corner of a garden hedge and continuing straight on across the field to a footbridge in the far hedge about 70 yards from the left-hand corner. Cross this, reentering Oxfordshire and take path LF1 straight on across the next field to a hedge gap in the far corner. Here cross a culvert and follow a right-hand fence straight on, bearing slightly right by an ash tree and continuing beside a right-hand ditch to gates onto the Little Faringdon road.

Turn left onto this road and after 250 yards turn right through gates onto bridleway LF1 following a stone farm road on the course of the old Fairford - Oxford railway for half a mile with views to your right towards Coleshill and Folly Hill. Eventually you pass through a gate and follow a grassy track along the old railway to a wooden bridlegate. Do **not** go through this, but turn left through an iron bridlegate and follow a right-hand hedge concealing Langford Brook for some 400 yards to reach a bridlebridge across the brook. Turn right over this passing through a bridlegate and take bridleway LA3 bearing half left across the next field to cross a culvert and go through a gate. Now follow the right-hand hedge for a quarter mile to the far side of the field. Here turn left along a grassy track beside a right-hand hedge. After 80 yards turn right through a hedge gap and follow a left-hand hedge, with Langford Church emerging from the trees ahead, to reach the far end of the field. Here turn right and take path LA5 beside a left-hand hedge for 70 yards, then turn left through a gate and take path LA3 beside a left-hand hedge to cross a stile at the far end of the field. Now bear half right across the next field to its far corner by Rectory Farm where you cross a concealed stile on the right-hand side of a stone garage and take Church Lane straight on to your starting point.

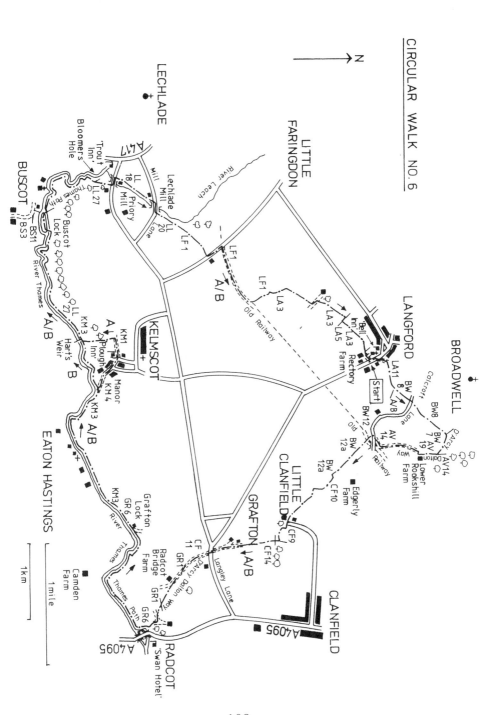

N

LECHLADE

LITTLE
FARINGDON

River Leach

BUSCOT

A417

Bloomers
Hole

Trout
Inn

LL
18

Priory
Mill

Lechlade
Mill

LL
27

Buscot
Lock

BS11

BS3

River Thames

Thames Path

LL 20

LF 1

LF1

LF1

A/B

Old Railway

LA3

LA3

LA3

LA5

Bell
Inn

Rectory
Farm

LANGFORD

BROADWELL

LA11

Start

Bw
8

A/B

Bw12

Colcroft

Bw8

Bw
7

AV
19

AV14

Dalton Way

Lower
Rookshill
Farm

AV
14

Bw
12a

Bw
12a

railway

old

Edgerly
Farm

CF10

KELMSCOT

Hart's
Weir

A

Plough
Inn

KM1

KM 4

Manor

KM3

A/B

B

A/B

LL 27

KM3

River Thames

EATON HASTINGS

KM3

Grafton
Lock

GR 6

River Thames

Camden
Farm

Radcot
Bridge
Farm

GR1

GR1

CF
11

GR1

Dalton Way

Langley Lane

LITTLE
CLANFIELD

CF9

CF14

GRAFTON

A/B

CLANFIELD

A4095

RADCOT

A4095

'Swan Hotel'

Thames Path

GR6

1km

1 mile

109

Circular Walk No. 7   Little Coxwell

Length of Walk: 8.1 miles / 13.1 Km
Starting Point: 'Eagle Tavern`, Little Coxwell.
Grid Ref: SU281934
Maps: OS Landranger Sheet 163 or 174
      OS Explorer Sheet 170
      OS Pathfinder Sheet 1135 (SU29/39)
How to get there / Parking: Little Coxwell, 1.5 miles south of
    Faringdon, may be reached from the town by taking the
    A417 towards Wantage, then turning right onto the A420
    towards Swindon. After 0.8 miles turn left onto the road
    to Fernham and Longcot, then after a further 0.4 miles
    turn right onto the road into Little Coxwell. Where the
    village street widens and the 'Eagle Tavern` comes into
    view ahead, park on the right. (NB The gravel strip on the
    left is private land where only permit-holders may park).

Little Coxwell, an estate village near a source of the River Ock called Cock Well, after which the village is named, can boast a tiny Norman church with a thirteenth-century bellcote. Since the opening of the Faringdon Bypass, Little Coxwell has been a cul-de-sac village which few outsiders visit whereas its namesake, Great Coxwell, through which the walk soon leads you, is very much on the tourist map due to its magnificent thirteenth-century tithe barn. This barn known as Great Barn was built by Cistercian monks from Beaulieu Abbey to house the parish tithes (a tax in kind of one-tenth of agricultural produce exacted from the ninth century onwards to pay for parish priests) which the Abbey received from local farmers after the Manor was given to it by King John in 1204. Donated to the National Trust in 1956, this Cotswold-stone barn, which is 152 feet long, is interesting both for its timber-framed interior construction and its sheer age as few agricultural buildings of this period have survived.

The walk, after passing through Great Coxwell, continues westwards to join the D´Arcy Dalton Way and follow it southwards by way of Coleshill where there are superb panoramic views towards the Cotswolds, Chilterns and Downs, eventually crossing the nascent River Ock and reaching Longcot. You then leave the D´Arcy Dalton Way and turn north, recrossing the Ock

and eventually passing Cock Well to return to Little Coxwell.

Starting with your back to the ´Eagle Tavern`, Little Coxwell, turn right past a telephone box, then right again along a road, soon ignoring a branching street to your right and two footpaths to your left, then bearing right and leaving the village. At the end of the road go straight on through a fence gap onto the A420, then turn right along its verge. After 40 yards between laybys turn left, crossing the road carefully and take macadamed path GC8 through a small gate and straight on across a golf course and a footbridge. Now continue across a field towards Great Coxwell with its thirteenth-century church with a fifteenth-century tower with fine views of the Downs to your left including White Horse Hill. At the far side of the field at the backs of gardens in Great Coxwell follow the macadam path bearing right then left into an alleyway leading to the village street opposite the Parish Reading Room dated 1900.

Here cross the road, turn right onto its footway and follow it past The Laurels and the post office, then, if wishing to visit the Great Barn, go straight on for another 250 yards. Otherwise, turn left into Puddleduck Lane going downhill and up again, leaving the village and now on bridleway GC11, continuing to gates into a farm. Here take a rough track straight on past the farm into a hedged lane and continue for nearly half a mile, ignoring branching tracks to right and left and eventually reaching a gate into a field. Now take bridleway CO9 along a stony track bearing slightly left across the field with fine views of the Downs to your left to pass through two gates in the far corner of the field. Here follow the track beside a left-hand fence to a gate onto a concrete farm road. Bear right onto this, soon passing through Colleymore Farm to reach the B4019.

Cross this road and take path CO12 straight on down the private road to Brimstone Farm. After a third of a mile, just before a sharp right-hand bend, turn left through a hedge gap onto path CO13 joining the D´Arcy Dalton Way and following a grassy track beside a right-hand hedge. Where the track bears right into Fern Copse, leave it and follow the edge of the wood to a field corner. Here cross a footbridge by an oak tree, then continue along the edge of the wood. By a corner of the wood, ignore a hedge gap to your right and follow a right-hand hedge uphill to the edge of Cuckoopen Plantation. Here turn right through a concealed hedge gap with superb views opening out ahead and to your right across Buscot Park and the Thames Valley towards the Cotswolds. Now follow the outside edge of the wood through two fields, gradually bearing left, then, where the wood edge bears right, turn left onto a fenced path through the wood to a gate and stile onto the B4019, where Coleshill village is a quarter mile to your right.

Coleshill, a hillside village named after the River Cole which forms the Wiltshire boundary, today boasts an attractive small green with the remains of an ancient cross and a much-restored Norman church with a fifteenth-century tower. Until 1952 Coleshill was an estate village ranged around a manor house built for Sir George Pratt between 1650 and 1662 to a design by the renowned architect Inigo Jones and said to be one of the latter's finest works, but, in that year the house, which had later passed to the Pleydell-Bouverie family, one of whom was made Earl of Radnor in 1765, was destroyed by fire and its ruins were demolished so that all that now remains are the park, gateposts, stables and a dovecot. Monuments to the Pleydell-Bouverie family can be found in the parish church, while the 'Radnor Arms' recalls their title and coat of arms.

Now cross the B4019 and turn left onto its verge, following the wall of Coleshill Park for over a quarter mile passing ornamental gates into the park. Soon after the woodland to your left ends and a superb view opens out towards Badbury Hill ahead and across Buscot Park and the Thames Valley towards the Cotswolds to your left, fork right onto bridleway CO10, the drive to Ashen Copse Farm, still beside the Coleshill Park wall with fine views soon opening out ahead towards the Downs and later Great Coxwell with its prominent church to your left. Having passed two fine cedars within the park walls and gates into the park, you finally leave the park behind and drop down to Ashen Copse Farm. Here ignore a crossing path and take the farm road straight on past the farm, soon losing its macadam surface, passing Ashen Copse Wood to your right and Ashen Copse Cottages to your left and continuing along a newly-planted avenue of trees to a hedge gap and culvert. Now on bridleway LT8, take a track gently uphill through avenues of newly-planted trees across two fields, then more steeply along a lane with sporadic hedges to reach Tithe Farm. Here keep right at a fork passing right of the buildings with a fine view of White Horse Hill opening out ahead, then bear left and continue along the farm road, now with fine views of Badbury Hill and Great Coxwell to your left and the Downs to your right in places, to reach the A420.

Cross this main road carefully and take the continuation of bridleway LT8 straight on through a hedge gap opposite, then between a right-hand fence and a line of posts with fine views towards the Downs ahead and Longcot with its prominent church tower to your left. Eventually the bridleway becomes enclosed first by a left-hand, then a right-hand hedge and you continue along a

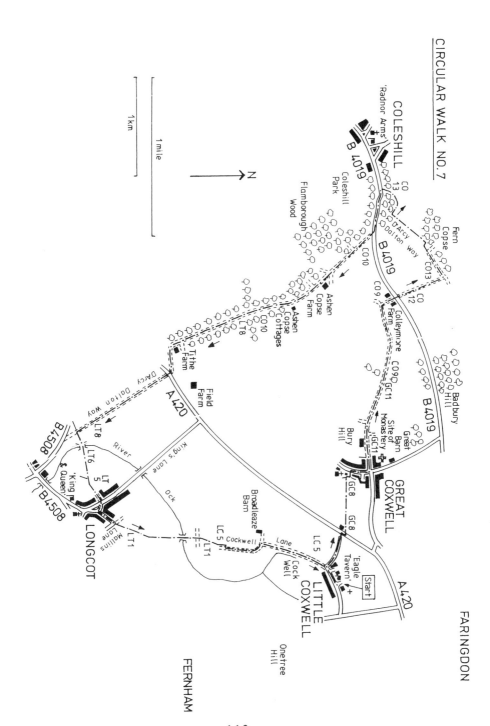

CIRCULAR WALK NO. 7

FARINGDON

FERNHAM

113

green lane for over a quarter mile, looking out for the footbridge of a crossing path to your left. Turn left over this bridge and a rail-stile onto path LT6, bearing slightly right across a field to a rail-stile and footbridge over the River Ock between clumps of willow trees, then bear half left across the next field, heading some way right of a thatched stone cottage at Longcot to cross a footbridge just left of the far corner of the field. Here turn left over a second footbridge and stile onto path LT5 following a right-hand hedge to cross a stile by a gate. Now continue across a small recreation ground and along a gravel track to reach King's Lane in Longcot.

Longcot, in the upper reaches of the Ock valley, offers fine views of Uffington's White Horse, which is of unknown origin but believed to date either from the Iron Age or the Saxon period. The thirteenth-century church with a kingpost roof and Jacobean pulpit, whose eighteenth-century tower is a landmark for miles around in this flat country, houses a memorial to Ernest Carter and his wife, Lilian, who drowned when the 'Titanic' sank in 1912. Although they did not live in Longcot, but in Whitechapel, East London, where Ernest was the vicar of St. Jude's Church, their memorial was moved here from Whitechapel by Lilian's uncle, John Hughes, the vicar of Longcot, when St. Jude's was demolished. Lilian, whose father was the writer Tom Hughes, well-known as author of 'Tom Brown's Schooldays', is also said to have been offered the last place in the last lifeboat to leave the 'Titanic' but to have declined in favour of someone else so as not to be separated from her husband.

Now bear half right across King's Lane and take a side-road called The Green. By a former pub turn sharp left into Mailin's Lane and follow it past a mixture of thatched cottages and modern houses. At a sharp right-hand bend turn left through the central of three hedge gaps and take path LT1 leaving a farm track and bearing half right across the field towards Onetree Hill to pass a corner of a left-hand hedge then bear slightly left to a gap in the far hedge. Here bear slightly right across the next field to a hedge gap where you cross a culvert over the Ock and follow a left-hand hedge. At the far side of this field cross some rails and a track and bear slightly right across the next field to cross a footbridge and stile. Now take path LC5 bearing slightly right across a corner of a field to cross a stile and footbridge by a wooden pylon leading to a farm road called Cockwell Lane. Turn left onto this and follow it for three-quarters of a mile, eventually passing Cock Well, a source of the Ock, and reaching the village street in Little Coxwell onto which you turn right and retrace your steps to the 'Eagle Tavern'.

Circular Walk No. 8   White Horse Hill

Length of Walk: 7.0 miles / 11.3 Km
Starting Point: Southern end of the main White Horse Hill car park at Woolstone Hill.
Grid Ref: SU293865
Maps: OS Landranger Sheet 174
OS Explorer Sheet 170
OS Pathfinder Sheet 1154 (SU28/38)
How to get there / Parking: Woolstone Hill, 6.5 miles west of Wantage, may be reached from the town by taking the winding B4507 towards Ashbury for nearly 7 miles until a brown signpost directs you left towards the car park for Uffington White Horse and Wayland´s Smithy, then follow this road up Woolstone Hill to the car park on the left.

White Horse Hill, at 856ft the highest point in Oxfordshire, is named after the Uffington White Horse on its north side which is generally believed to be about 2000 years old and the oldest of the fifteen such horses in England, although some think it only dates from Saxon times. Its prominence as a local landmark has resulted in the Ock valley below becoming known as the Vale of the White Horse and in 1974 this also became the name of the local district council. Even older than the White Horse is the large, well-preserved hillfort known as Uffington Castle which encloses some eight acres of the hilltop and is believed to date from 500 B.C., while Dragon Hill to the north is variously said to be the site of St. George´s slaying of the dragon or the burial place of Uther Pendragon, father of King Arthur.

The walk leads you from the car park over the summit of White Horse Hill, with its hillfort and superb panoramic views, to reach the Ridgeway, before turning to descend the north side of the hill, passing between the strange-looking Dragon Hill and a spectacular coombe called The Manger to reach the Icknield Way. You then continue downhill to the valley floor before turning west through the picturesque villages of Woolstone and Compton Beauchamp, joining the D´Arcy Dalton Way and following it back up the Downs to its terminus at the ancient barrow called Wayland´s Smithy. From here your return route takes the ancient Ridgeway along the crest of the Downs to

Woolstone Hill where you descend back to the car park.

Starting from the far end of Woolstone Hill car park, climb a flight of steps to a picnic area where you pass through two gates and bear half right across open downland towards the top of White Horse Hill with a good view of the White Horse slightly to your left and panoramic views on a clear day across much of Oxfordshire and parts of Berkshire, Wiltshire, Gloucestershire and Bucks, to reach a cairn with a direction-finder erected by the Royal Military College of Science in Shrivenham to mark the Queen's Silver Jubilee in 1977. Here keep straight on to a gate onto Dragonhill Road. Cross this road and a sleeper-bridge opposite, then take a worn path straight on to a dip in the ramparts of Uffington Castle where fresh views towards Berkshire open out ahead. Now go straight on across the hillfort to pass through a dip in its far side, then bear left along a grassy track beside the Ridgeway fence to reach a bridlegate leading onto the Ridgeway, thought to be at least 5000 years old and thus one of the most ancient highways in the world.

Here turn left onto the Ridgeway (UF23) with fine views ahead towards Didcot Power Station and the Chilterns and to your right towards Berkshire. After 250 yards turn left over a stile onto path UF22, following a right-hand fence with fine views to your right at first, then later also ahead. Where the fence turns right, leave it and bear slightly right, passing just right of two stunted trees and entering a sunken way. Follow this, bearing left and dropping steeply to pass a steep-sided coombe to your right and descend a flight of steps onto Dragonhill Road. Now take path WS6 opposite towards the strange-looking, flat-topped knoll known as Dragon Hill, then forking left to pass left of Dragon Hill and skirt the top of the spectacular left-hand coombe known as The Manger to reach a gate and stile where you should turn round for a view of the White Horse from below. Having crossed the stile, bear half right leaving the coombe and crossing a slight rise to a stile, then go straight on downhill to a gate and stile onto the B4507, Icknield Way.

Turn right onto this road with a further view of the White Horse to your right. After 350 yards, at a crossroads, turn left onto the Uffington and Faringdon road and descend for half a mile, passing Sower Hill Farm to your left and ignoring a branching path to your right. After the road has levelled out, disregard a second branching path to your right, then turn left over a stile by gates onto path UF20 following a right-hand hedge through two fields and a small plantation. Now cross a stile and take path WS13 beside a left-hand hedge straight on through two fields with views towards Uffington to your right with its unusual octagonal church tower. At the far end of the second field cross a stile by gates to reach a road on the edge of Woolstone and bear slightly left onto it, following it through this picturesque village with its timber-framed and thatched cottages and a tiny twelfth-century church.

At a road junction by the 'White Horse' inn go straight on, then at a sharp right-hand bend by Upper Farm, take path WS14 straight on up a drive, bearing slightly left to cross a stile right of double gates. Now follow the left-hand hedge through two fields to a stile onto byway CB12, Hardwell Lane. Turn left into this thousand-year-old lane then immediately right over a footbridge and stile onto path CB5, bearing left across the corner of a field to a stile at the corner of a belt of scrub. Now follow the right-hand fence straight on past the moated Hardwell Farm to your right with fine views to your right across the Vale towards Coleshill and Badbury Hill and later ahead towards Swindon. At the far end of the field cross a stile and follow a left-hand hedge straight on to a stile where you join the D'Arcy Dalton Way and bear half left to a currently redundant stile onto Knighton Road on the edge of Knighton. Turn right onto this road, then immediately left through a gate onto bridleway CB2 and follow a left-hand tree-belt through two fields. Where the tree-belt ends, take a grassy track straight on to a gate onto a bend in Shrivenham Road at Compton Beauchamp.

Compton Beauchamp, in its sheltered leafy hollow at the foot of the Downs, today comprises little more than a church, a manor house and a row of cottages, the majority of its parishioners living in the nearby hamlet of Knighton. The imposing Compton House is of Georgian appearance but is understood to be older while the nearby church of St. Swithun dates from the thirteenth century and has a squat fifteenth-century tower, its main treasure being some fine fourteenth-century glass. Its relatively rare dedication to the Saxon, St. Swithun, famous for his saint's day whose weather is said to be indicative of the rest of the summer, however, suggests that the present church replaced an earlier building.

Take Shrivenham Road straight on past the drive to Compton House to your left, then, at a right-hand bend, take the road to the church straight on. At a fork keep right, passing a barn with a clock tower and continuing along macadam path CB1 to gates to the tiny whitewashed church. Here turn right through a hunting gate and follow the churchyard fence at first, then bear slightly left across the field to a gate. Now bear half right across the next field past a corner of Home Copse to your right, crossing a wooden fence and continuing to a hedge gap in the far corner of the field. Here take path AS7 straight on by a left-hand hedge through two fields with fine views across the Vale towards Swindon ahead and Shrivenham, Watchfield and Coleshill to your right. In the second field follow the hedge, bearing left at one point, then, where it ends, bear slightly right across the field to a footbridge and stiles in the valley bottom. Now take a fenced track straight on uphill by a left-hand hedge to the top corner of the right-hand field where you join bridleway AS20 and go along a short green lane to a gate and stile. Here turn left through a second gate and soon bear slightly left to reach a farm road which you follow gently uphill past Odstone Farm, ignoring a crossing farm road and continuing with views to your right into Wiltshire towards Charlbury Hill and Swindon to reach the B4507. Cross this road bearing slightly right and take AS19, a sunken way through scrub up Odstone Hill. On leaving the scrub, it is worth climbing the right-hand bank to the stile of a branching path for fine views across three counties (Oxfordshire, Wiltshire and Gloucestershire). Now continue along the sunken way which soon merges with a farm road, then follow this straight on for a third of a mile with fine views over your right shoulder similar to those from the stile and to your left towards Wayland's Smithy in its clump of trees. On reaching the Ridgeway (AS18), turn left onto it and follow it for nearly 300 yards, then turn left through gates and take a fenced permissive path to Wayland's Smithy.

Wayland's Smithy, which may be older than the Ridgeway itself, is a well-preserved Neolithic chambered long barrow believed to date from about 3400 B.C. built over an earlier barrow thought to be some 300 years older and now surrounded by a ring of trees. Its name is, however, of Saxon origin deriving from a mythical smith called Weland. Legend has it that if a horse which has lost a shoe is left tethered at the Smithy for ten minutes, a silver coin is left and the rider whistles three times, Weland will shoe the horse and take the silver in payment. First opened in 1919, the Smithy was further excavated and restored to its present condition in 1962-3.

Now retrace your steps to the Ridgeway (AS18) and turn left onto it, soon with views opening out towards White Horse Hill ahead and the Lambourn valley to your right, famous for its race-horse training. Now on CB11 go straight on, crossing a narrow road called Knighton Hill, ignoring a branching path to your left and eventually (now on WS3) reaching a rough crossing road. Turn left onto this towards Woolstone and follow it for 400 yards. On reaching a bend in a macadam road, go straight on down Woolstone Hill for 300 yards to the car park on your right.

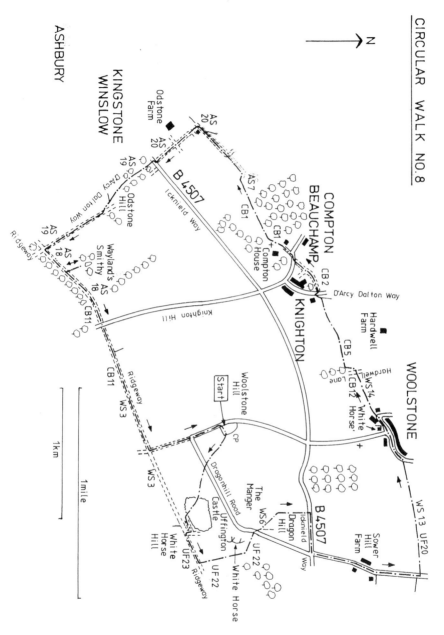

CIRCULAR WALK NO.8

N

ASHBURY

KINGSTONE
WINSLOW

Odstone
Farm

AS
20

AS
20

AS
19

D'Arcy Dalton Way

Odstone
Hill

AS
19

AS
18

Wayland's
Smithy

AS
18

Ridgeway

CB11

CB11

Ridgeway
WS 3

WS 3

WS 3

B 4507

Icknield Way

CB1

CB1

Compton
House

AS 7

COMPTON
BEAUCHAMP

CB 2

D'Arcy Dalton Way

KNIGHTON

Knighton Hill

Hardwell
Farm

CB5

Hardwell Lane

CB12

WS 14

White
Horse

WOOLSTONE

Start

Woolstone
Hill

CP

Dragonhill Road

Castle
Uffington

White
Horse
Hill

Ridgeway

UF23

UF 22

White Horse

UF 22

The
Manger

WS6

Dragon
Hill

Icknield Way

B 4507

+

Sower
Hill
Farm

WS 13 UF20

UFFINGTON

1km

1mile

119

INDEX OF PLACE NAMES

(DW : D´Arcy Dalton Way Map No. / CW : Circular Walk)

(DW : D'Arcy Dalton Way Map No. / CW : Circular Walk)

Books Published by
THE BOOK CASTLE

**COUNTRYSIDE CYCLING IN BEDFORDSHIRE,
BUCKINGHAMSHIRE AND HERTFORDSHIRE**: Mick Payne.
Twenty rides on- and off-road for all the family.

**PUB WALKS FROM COUNTRY STATIONS:
Bedfordshire and Hertfordshire**: Clive Higgs.
Fourteen circular country rambles, each starting and finishing at a
railway station and incorporating a pub-stop at a mid-way point.

**PUB WALKS FROM COUNTRY STATIONS:
Buckinghamshire and Oxfordshire:** Clive Higgs.
Circular rambles incorporating pub-stops.

LOCAL WALKS: South Bedfordshire and North Chilterns:
Vaughan Basham.
Twenty-seven thematic circular walks.

LOCAL WALKS: North and Mid Bedfordshire: Vaughan Basham.
Twenty-five thematic circular walks.

FAMILY WALKS: Chilterns South: Nick Moon.
Thirty 3 to 5 mile circular walks.

FAMILY WALKS: Chilterns North: Nick Moon.
Thirty shorter circular walks.

**CHILTERN WALKS: Hertfordshire, Bedfordshire and
North Buckinghamshire**: Nick Moon.
CHILTERN WALKS: Buckinghamshire: Nick Moon.
**CHILTERN WALKS: Oxfordshire and
West Buckinghamshire**: Nick Moon.
A trilogy of circular walks, in association with the Chiltern Society.
Each volume contains 30 circular walks.

**OXFORDSHIRE WALKS: Oxford, the Cotswolds and the
Cherwell Valley**: Nick Moon.
**OXFORDSHIRE WALKS: Oxford, the Downs and
the Thames Valley**: Nick Moon.
Two volumes that complement Chiltern Walks: Oxfordshire and
complete coverage of the county, in association with the Oxford
Fieldpaths Society. Thirty circular walks in each.

JOURNEYS INTO BEDFORDSHIRE: Anthony Mackay.
Foreword by The Marquess of Tavistock, Woburn Abbey. A lavish book of over 150 evocative ink drawings.

JOURNEYS INTO BUCKINGHAMSHIRE: Anthony Mackay
Superb line drawings plus background text: large format landscape gift book.

BUCKINGHAMSHIRE MURDERS: Len Woodley
Nearly two centuries of nasty crimes.

HISTORIC FIGURES IN THE BUCKINGHAMSHIRE LANDSCAPE: John Houghton.
Major personalities and events that have shaped the county's past, including a special section on Bletchley Park.

TWICE UPON A TIME: John Houghton.
Short stories loosely based on fact, set in the North Bucks area.

**MANORS and MAYHEM, PAUPERS and PARSONS:
Tales from Four Shires: Beds., Bucks., Herts., and Northants.**:
John Houghton
Little-known historical snippets and stories.

**MYTHS and WITCHES, PEOPLE and POLITICS:
Tales from Four Shires: Bucks., Beds., Herts., and Northants.**:
John Houghton.
Anthology of strange, but true historical events.

FOLK: Characters and Events in the History of Bedfordshire and Northamptonshire: Vivienne Evans.
Anthology about people of yesteryear – arranged alphabetically by village or town.

JOHN BUNYAN: His Life and Times: Vivienne Evans.
Highly-praised and readable account.

THE RAILWAY AGE IN BEDFORDSHIRE: Fred Cockman.
Classic, illustrated account of early railway history.

GLEANINGS REVISITED: Nostalgic Thoughts of a Bedfordshire Farmer's Boy: E W O'Dell.
His own sketches and early photographs adorn this lively account of rural Bedfordshire in days gone by.

BEDFORDSHIRE'S YESTERYEARS Vol 2: The Rural Scene:
Brenda Fraser-Newstead.
Vivid first-hand accounts of country life two or three generations ago.

BEDFORDSHIRE'S YESTERYEARS Vol 3:
Craftsmen and Tradespeople: Brenda Fraser-Newstead.
Fascinating recollections over several generations practising many vanishing crafts and trades.

BEDFORDSHIRE'S YESTERYEARS Vol 4:
War Times and Civil Matters: Brenda Fraser-Newstead.
Two World Wars, plus transport, law and order, etc.

DUNSTABLE WITH THE PRIORY: 1100–1550: Vivienne Evans.
Dramatic growth of Henry I's important new town around a major crossroads.

DUNSTABLE IN TRANSITION: 1550–1700: Vivienne Evans.
Wealth of original material as the town evolves without the Priory.

DUNSTABLE DECADE: THE EIGHTIES:
A Collection of Photographs: Pat Lovering.
A souvenir book of nearly 300 pictures of people and events in the 1980s.

DUNSTABLE IN DETAIL: Nigel Benson.
A hundred of the town's buildings and features, plus town trail map.

OLD DUNSTABLE: Bill Twaddle.
A new edition of this collection of early photographs.

BOURNE and BRED: A Dunstable Boyhood Between the Wars:
Colin Bourne.
An elegantly written, well-illustrated book capturing the spirit of the town over fifty years ago.

ROYAL HOUGHTON: Pat Lovering:
Illustrated history of Houghton Regis from the earliest times to the present.

THE STOPSLEY BOOK: James Dyer.
Definitive, detailed account of this historic area of Luton. 150 rare photographs.

PUBS and PINTS: The Story of Luton's Public Houses
and Breweries: Stuart Smith.
The background to beer in the town, plus hundreds of photographs, old and new.

THE CHANGING FACE OF LUTON: An Illustrated History:
Stephen Bunker, Robin Holgate and Marian Nichols.
Luton's development from earliest times to the present busy industrial town. Illustrated in colour and mono.

WHERE THEY BURNT THE TOWN HALL DOWN:
Luton, The First World War and the Peace Day Riots, July 1919:
Dave Craddock.
Detailed analysis of a notorious incident.

THE MEN WHO WORE STRAW HELMETS:
Policing Luton, 1840–1974: Tom Madigan.
Meticulously chronicled history; dozens of rare photographs; author
served in Luton Police for fifty years.

BETWEEN THE HILLS:
The Story of Lilley, a Chiltern Village: Roy Pinnock.
A priceless piece of our heritage – the rural beauty remains but the
customs and way of life described here have largely disappeared.

KENILWORTH SUNSET:
A Luton Town Supporter's Journal: Tim Kingston.
Frank and funny account of football's ups and downs.

A HATTER GOES MAD!:
Kristina Howells.
Luton Town footballers, officials and supporters talk to a female fan.

LEGACIES:
Tales and Legends of Luton and the North Chilterns:
Vic Lea.
Twenty-five mysteries and stories based on fact, including Luton
Town Football Club. Many photographs.

LEAFING THROUGH LITERATURE:
Writers' Lives in Hertfordshire and Bedfordshire:
David Carroll.
Illustrated short biographies of many famous authors and their
connections with these counties.

A PILGRIMAGE IN HERTFORDSHIRE: H M Alderman.
Classic, between-the-wars tour round the county, embellished with
line drawings.

SUGAR MICE AND STICKLEBACKS:
Childhood Memories of a Hertfordshire Lad: Harry Edwards
Vivid evocation of those gentler pre-war days in an archetypal village,
Hertingfordbury.

SWANS IN MY KITCHEN: Lis Dorer.
Story of a Swan Sanctuary near Hemel Hempstead.

THE HILL OF THE MARTYR:
An Architectural History of St. Albans Abbey: Eileen Roberts.
Scholarly and readable chronological narrative history of Hertfordshire and Bedfordshire's famous cathedral. Fully illustrated with photographs and plans.

CHILTERN ARCHAEOLOGY: RECENT WORK:
A Handbook for the Next Decade: edited by Robin Holgate.
The latest views, results and excavations by twenty-three leading archaeologists throughout the Chilterns.

THE TALL HITCHIN INSPECTOR'S CASEBOOK:
A Victorian Crime Novel Based on Fact: Edgar Newman.
Worthies of the time encounter more archetypal villains.

SPECIALLY FOR CHILDREN

VILLA BELOW THE KNOLLS: A Story of Roman Britain: Michael Dundrow.
An exciting adventure for young John in Totternhoe and Dunstable two thousand years ago.

THE RAVENS: One Boy Against the Might of Rome: James Dyer.
On the Barton Hills and in the south-east of England as the men of the great fort of Ravensburgh (near Hexton) confront the invaders.

Books Distributed by THE BOOK CASTLE

Further titles are in preparation.

All the above are available via any bookshop, or from the publisher and bookseller,

THE BOOK CASTLE
12 Church Street, Dunstable, Bedfordshire, LU5 4RU
Tel: (01582) 605670